Country Acres

Country Acres

Country Wisdom for the Working Landscape

David Larkin

with Sabra Elliott Larkin

A David Larkin Book

Houghton Mifflin Company

Boston New York 1998

For information about this and other Houghton Mifflin trade and
reference books and multimedia productions, visit The Bookstore at
Houghton Mifflin on the World Wide Web at http://www.hmco.com/trade/.

CIP data is available

"Watering Trough" (excerpt), copyright © 1970 by Maxine Kumin,
from *Selected Poems 1960-1990* by Maxine Kumin. Reprinted
by permission of W. W. Norton & Company, Inc.

Printed in Italy

SFE 10 9 8 7 6 5 4 3 2 1

*Nature's
insecticide.
A ladybug will
consume fifty
aphids a day.*

Contents

Introduction

I am looking out the kitchen door and up the field to the path that leads through the woods to our pond. It is Michaelmas, the last of September, when vegetation stops growing and when, traditionally, back in the English country-side, the grass-eating goose was brought in to be fed on grain in preparation for the Christmas feast. For me it means the end of mowing the meadow; I can put the lawn tractor away. A quick glance is all I need to remind me of what else has to be done, and at this time of the year the doing itself is a pleasure. The temperature is just right for work outdoors, and the foliage is a mixture of summer and fall colors.

In the middle distance is the raspberry patch. The canes must be pruned better than they were last year; I didn't cut them short enough, and the heavy snowfall bent and flattened them, worse even than when a bear squashed the patch getting at the fruit one summer night. Poking through the woods are unpruned, unsprayed, old apple trees — beyond care but still producing. Everything is edged with Michaelmas daisies, which the Shakers used as a medicine for skin complaints.

Along the path rising to the woods is a line of blueberry bushes planted by my wife to bear fruit from early summer through September. Now, in their fifth year, her patience has been rewarded. Every couple of weeks the berries on succeeding bushes have ripened one by one. Today the last bush is full of fruit.

Immediately in the foreground is our stream and the trout fingerlings that have made it this far up. Three years ago I improvised a way to catch them in isolated pools. Wearing my wrap-around angler's sunglasses, I looked like a mad scientist as I stood in the stream peering down and, using two plastic dust pans, periodically scooped baby trout into a bucket. I then carried them up to our pond where they grew to be a food source.

As I think about it, I'm surprised that the very simple scenes I've just described are so full of information. The descriptions of middle distance and foreground sound like attempts to describe a picture because, for me, retaining visual information is how I learn and remember. I wonder how other newcomers to country acres think about their properties and the possibilities for change, for we each have the chance to make our personal imprint on the land we own.

One of the most popular paintings in Britain's National Gallery is *The Haywain* by John Constable. It's a summer landscape of a mill, a placid river, fields of hay in the distance, and a busy sky suggesting a breeze and a change of weather. Right in the middle of the picture, and in midstream, is a wagon — the haywain of the title — with its team of shire horses and a pair of young lads idling their noonday time. This composition was not arranged by the artist for its pictorial quality alone, it was an accurately observed scene of rural life and work. The reason carts were rested in the water was so that their wooden wheels would swell. A busy day of hay making, heat, and rough fields and roads could separate an iron tire from its rim, which might even work loose, causing the wheel to collapse under the weight of some three tons of hay. Also, the hooves of the horses were feathered and often became clogged with dirt and mud, which led to a disease called "greasy heel." Horses' legs also heated up from heavy pulling. In this painting the young lads rest the team, literally cooling their heels. This could hardly be a modern scene, since tractors don't need to cool off in a stream bed. But compared with cities and their suburbs, the working countryside changes very little.

John Constable, Jean François Millet, and Vincent Van Gogh were all country boys. These artists found no reason to rearrange the essentials depicted in their paintings.

The Haywain,
by John Constable.
The National Gallery,
London.

From Millet we feel what it was like to sow miles of seed by hand and, later in the year, to bend over for hours until dark, picking grains enough to make a loaf of bread. Van Gogh painted every tool and implement of the French farm; farm work was the main subject of his career. Of the many more references in painting, closest to where I live are the primitive examples by Grandma Moses, who started painting at the age of 78 — not from observation but from memory. She gives us a wealth of country and farming information, although a bit rose-colored. Even so, I doubt that the scenes she painted of the Hoosick and Battenkill valleys are today very different in appearance or population. Such pictures are packed with history — they are the documentaries of farming life of not so long ago. I don't want to suggest that information transcends art, but for an illustrated book such as this one we can look at these paintings as colored postcards from the past, reminders of the unchanging character of the working landscape.

Unfortunately, the quality of the land can be its own undoing. The Amish, for example, know where the good land is, and they farm it in a traditional manner. People admire the natural ways of Amish farming life and want to move to such an idyllic spot. They buy homes, up go the prices, and away go the Amish. Towns were made to be towns, but a suburb is no more than country that has been encroached upon.

Cities with parks, avenues, cemeteries, and manicured lawns don't connect us to the country. They teach us little about growing flowers or produce, or about the land's capacity for renewal. But to some extent the city dweller can invent the country. My eldest daughter now lives in the heart of London, three-quarters of a mile from the Houses of Parliament. She is lucky to have a tiny back garden with her flat. Immediately after moving in she started to grow her kitchen herbs and planted a bay tree. Climbing plants were instructed to grow around the door. There is even a stone path leading to the back gate and a lawn the size of a dining table, just large enough for deck chairs. Though my daughter and I never discussed this,

it was a wonderful example of a rooted interest in rural living.

The move to a rural life is influenced by one's attitude toward it. My wife and I, for example, felt sure that the improving state of communications would enable us to be just as productive professionally in the country as we were in the city, and have a healthy life surrounded by nature as well. Some non-farming Americans see the country in terms of wildness, and support the need to conserve it so they can play on it later; others, Europeans in particular, look upon it in the manner of people more familiar with the farming landscape — as something worth saving as it is.

I think the prospect of owning the land itself is just as exciting as having a country house. Some of us, when we see how much acreage we have — and the potential work involved — decide to "let it go back to nature for a while." You can be sure that the process was already well under way. Eventually, however, most of us have a go at working the land. Some of us sell our timber and in the process become tree farmers. Many are slow to make improvements such as repairing fences, creating paths, or digging a pond. But it doesn't take long to see the benefits of putting the land back to work. One can sow a field into pasture, for example, then have it mowed and fertilized by a neighboring farmer's herd. Or one can make hay just to keep the brush down.

In America there is still the call of the wild; people think about self-sufficiency and a return to the roots of the first pioneering culture. There are flexible minds here, and it's not difficult to think about changing one's living environment. People who move to the country form a strong attachment to the land. Class differences become meaningless as people from all walks of life share their love of the land and information about it. But this book is certainly not an argument in support of self-sufficiency. It's for those who are thinking about a move, and for those already here who want to be reminded of the many ways we can partake of the rich and rewarding life of the country.

The farming landscape

Cultivated fields, with their furrows and ditches, are what we see on the approach to the farmyard and its buildings. They present a kind of natural architecture. To understand how fields emerged from the landscape, we must return to the time when animals were domesticated and kept for their meat, milk, skins, and wool, as well as their use for farm work. Animals were valued, needed some husbandry, and had to be fenced in. There was no need to enclose corn — it wasn't going to wander across the road. Today the patchworks of fields we see are where the arable has replaced the pastoral. Walls and fences now serve to mark the boundaries of property. What seem to be hedges in the eastern U.S. are usually overgrown stone walls. The building of such walls required a great deal of effort, and removal was equally difficult, so as farming changed they remained as archaeological evidence and tree covered windbreaks. Sometimes the trees that live amongst the walls are the oldest on the farm, left as boundary markers or for plowmen to use to line up their teams. Where I live, large maples often survive in rows along the old boundaries, a sap tube linking the trees to the sugarhouse below as it ties the working landscape together.

A change in farming came about when farmers learned the virtues of interchanging livestock and crops on the same land. The farmer preferred to raise grains, but sheep and cattle, while grazing on fallow land, enriched it with manure. Better humus came from fields used as pasture land than from the leaf mold of the surrounding woods; hence more fields were made.

It's easy to follow the work of the farmer as he cleared the woodland. We can see where work stopped, where enough stumps were taken out, where enough stones were collected to make the walls needed for a field of a particular size. Wherever the land flattens out in our own valley, the fields get bigger. Fields are smaller on steep slopes, then larger again on the high crests of the hills. Throughout history farmers have looked for land where manageable fields slope as gently as possible to the south.

Furrows follow contour lines, then swing out as the plow turns.

Corn in late August at the bottom of our hill. Every patch of soil is used for growing.

Winter wheat coming through in mid-August.

Field shapes with ancient hedges, evolving from how the terrain and the plow divided up the land.

The invention of the plow also helped give the typical field its size and proportion. Once a team of oxen was harnessed and moving, a lot of energy was required to turn and reverse direction. The fewer turns the oxen had to make the better. It was a natural outcome that early fields were mostly rectangular in shape. The length of the furrow after turning the team gave us the word "furlong" (1/8 of a mile, or 201 meters).

Before the development of crop rotation and furrowing, agriculture was in the form of communal strip farming. Few peasant families could afford a team of oxen, so they were borrowed from the more prosperous among them. There was no property ownership then, so villagers divided up strips of the best land and repaid the ox owner at harvest time. Eventually all peasant land became enclosed and boundaries firm. A typical early farm was about thirty acres. The word acre originates from the amount of land that a team could plow in a day.

The farms of New England reflect both the habits and field sizes of the Old World. Even with so much land available, there was a limit to the amount of work that could be done by one family. The first settlers felt they were a civilized people and enclosed themselves and their cattle for protection from wild beasts and wild natives. The cattle would be tethered by day; wheat would be grown communally. Fears subsided and confidence grew. The developed New England terrain began to resemble the landscapes of Derbyshire, Yorkshire, and Wales.

The first fields in the New World looked like those of the Old. They rarely had straight boundaries; they followed the line of the plowman as he swung out to make the turn. New machinery and the Homestead Act soon helped to make the fields straight.

A fallow field outside the neat fencing and squared-up buildings of an early 1900s' Iowa farm.

In the South, for different reasons, it was back to strip farming. Here the developers had moved in early and saw fertile soil and slow-moving, navigable rivers as the way to prosperity if one could obtain river frontage and a landing. Many of the early farms and plantations were very narrow. A few hundred yards of river bank frontage might then stretch back past the house for more than a mile. And from each landing off went indigo, rice, tobacco, and later, cotton. On such level ground, the lower the field, the longer the season; and being near the coast, a large lake, or a wide river, the soil will be less affected by late spring or early fall frosts. Up in the high ground, where there are dips, bowls, and vales, frost pockets form as cold air flows like water from higher to lower levels and becomes trapped.

Today, as the Amish in Lancaster County, Pennsylvania, and Polish potato-farming families on the eastern forks of Long Island have found, good farmland attracts people who eventually kill it off. On Long Island, however, a five-acre plot surrounded by second homes has supported many market gardeners from a farming background who have been clever enough to raise seasonal fruits and vegetables. A few newcomers have even discovered that this rich, light soil just above sea level is like the wide Gironde estuary of Bordeaux, France, and have become vineyard owners. They jealously guard their piece of Eden from developers and protest energetically against further invasion. But most often, as in other farming areas where developers have moved in and partitioned the land, the adaptable buildings remain.

Buildings

Living here in America, immigrants from Europe remembered farmyards with buildings set around a muddy square, or in a row, one against the wall of the next. In America the availability of space and timber often resulted in collections of structures that appeared — to the European eye — to have been dropped gently from space. The whole scene bespeaks a kind of confidence, a sense of independence and openness as if to say, "We don't care what we look like." The only boundaries might be a picket fence around the farm's vegetable garden and orchard, or perhaps a fenced stock pen. In many of today's suburbs, deliberately repetitive landscaping and identical front lawns give the impression of a conforming society. A cluster of American farm buildings has the opposite effect — it exhibits a very real sense of freedom in its disposition.

The farmyard layout may seem indiscriminate at first. It is difficult to know the order in which buildings were constructed and why they were placed where they were, until an understanding of the strategy emerges. The barn, for example, is likely to have been the farthest of the working buildings from the dangerous sparks of the house chimney. The very old farms were designed along the track connecting them to the next settlement, so the entrances faced on the road on both sides.

An old barn would have its big doors facing the prevailing wind to make threshing easier. If there was a slope, the farmer might use it to provide a barn foundation and to create space for cattle stalls so that hay and feed could be driven in and dropped down from the level above. The dairy would be near the house, but the smokehouse and privy were maintained at a respectable distance.

Sometimes it takes a bit of thought and experience to decide what a particular building was designed for. If there was no barn, at least there would be a structure that once served as a wagon shed, carriage house, or a stable, and ended up a garage-cum-woodshed. Nearly every farmhouse grew lean-to additions, or ells. In the Northeast, in Maine and New Hampshire, the linear habit of Northern England took root again. Later, as farms became more organized, buildings were linked together joining the main house, little house, back house, and barn for comfort and efficiency. In most parts of the country, however, they remained quite separate, even though in some cases connected by a dogtrot or other such device. As farming changed, buildings large and small were left in place and used for another purpose or left to fall down. Nearly every old property has on it, along with the house, the foundation of another building of some kind. There was once a barn on our place, two hundred yards from our house, right on the road.

Farm buildings in America can be roughly divided into two groups, vernacular and folk. The vernacular are workaday buildings around a farm that illustrated its growth and established its size or even its decline. Most standing stables, carriage houses, cribs, sheds, barns, and other outbuildings don't show the history, roots, or culture of a particular farm family. They likely date from the mid-19th century and follow plans obtained by suppliers, or were put up by local builders with one tried-and-true style — commonplace, but well built and designed. Contemporary vernacular farm buildings are steel framed and aluminum sided, or constructed of cinder block, both standing on poured concrete. Any wood framing would likely consist of kiln-dried 2-by-4's.

The other group is what has been called folk architecture. This is truly local, using local materials and often built by the first farmers themselves with absolutely no plans, just the firmly implanted traditions and styles of the Old Country.

Whether vernacular or folk, the working structures on a farm needed a lot more ventilation than did the house: the hay barracks, corncribs, and barns to keep the contents dry; the springhouse to keep the water cool; the dairy to keep the milk and cream from spoiling. The stables, pigpens, and chicken houses needed fresh air for the health of the animals. These requirements meant that the buildings were very cold in the winter. Today they frustrate many who want to use such buildings for living and work, since their infrastructure makes insulation difficult and expensive.

The "old log cabin" was first brought to America by the Scandinavians and Germans. Both nationalities used the same nailless method, but re-created the sizes and shapes they were used to. The Scotch-Irish settlers borrowed these styles but kept the floor plans and sizes of their former stone and thatched cottages.

A sturdy **barn**, usually the first permanent building to be constructed when families moved to new land, became the heart of the farm. It was essential for survival to shelter the animals and to protect grain and food during the winter. The barn often was constructed with better timbers and other materials than was the house. The first American barns were based on the medieval European barn, which had a wide center aisle, high roof, and narrow aisles set off by supporting columns, similar to the basilica of an early Christian church. The center aisle became the barn's threshing floor, while the side aisles became space for storing hay and for animal stalls. It was then adapted by different groups of settlers to be more functional in the varying climates and landscapes of the colonies.

English settlers in New England in the 17th and 18th centuries, for example, introduced a barn with a side entry. This style and its variations can be found throughout Canada and the U.S. Constructed of wood, brick, or stone, with three bays, the English barn has the wagon door at the center of the long wall, and the threshing floor running the width — rather than the length — of the interior.

The Pennsylvania bank barn became an archetypal American barn. It was inspired by barns in mountainous Switzerland and Bavaria, where farmers built them into the slopes. In the New World they utilized the same technique, building on a stone foundation and into the side of a hill — hence the name "bank." The bottom level allowed animals and wagons easy access to the yard, and the top level provided separate space for grain storage.

Two views of a small Wyoming barn in winter.

This 1850s' English-style barn in Minnesota was built with the up-to-date features like the row of transom windows above the door. The fencing is made of local tamarack logs.

A small carriage-house barn in Salem County, New Jersey.

The roof, the most important element of the barn,
determines both the interior and exterior character of
the building. The covering material was first thatch, then
wood, and eventually shingle. The original pitched roof
is still the most common, although later it was often
modified into the gambrel roof that provided extra
storage needed by larger farms. Ventilating cupolas and
weather vanes became two of the distinctive and useful
additions to the roofs of large barns.

As standards of hygiene rose, the milking parlor was separated from the stalls. Some well-designed cow barns became obsolete when larger cows were needed to make dairying economical — the Holstein became the breed chosen for milk production. I saw a fine barn just a few years ago that had just thirty stalls. They were too short for Holsteins, whose back legs would have stood in the manure gutter. It seemed a sad end to a great building not designed to cope with current methods.

Very early on, farmers realized that domesticated cattle had lost the ability to lead the open-air life of wild animals, and needed shelter. Before there were milking parlors, a fine day meant that the cow could be milked outdoors. It also meant that the milk would be cleaner, if we consider the state of cowsheds then. Like the stable, the cowshed and calf shed were near the house, convenient to the kitchen.

Above. An old cowshed in Denmark. Many early American barns had first floors laid out like this.

Left. A brick cattle-shed barn in Holland built as the extension to a "long house"— the farmer's living quarters at one end of the structure shared the same roofline.

23

Previous page. In 1836, a carriage barn was added on the end of the 1750 parsonage built for the Reverend Adonijah Bidwell. Today it serves as a shed, complete with drying racks, for the 19th-century tools and implements used in the working vegetable garden that specializes in heirloom varieties.

In deep Wyoming snow the flock cannot survive without being in the farmyard.

These orphan lambs would have been farmyard-raised.

The animals needing the least housing or cover were the sheep, originally kept for their milk and mutton. Fleece was considered a bonus. As clothing for all improved in the Middle Ages, there was an increased need for wool, and the hardy sheep became a valuable animal of the hills. In both the Old World and the New, farmers worried about the flock only during lambing time, which always occurred in the harsh days of late winter and very early spring. A shelter or fold often was built onto an existing stone wall in the usually rocky, remote terrain to give protection to birthing ewes and the lonely shepherd. In the warmer lowland all the flock needed was a windbreak, and the shepherd had his cottage nearby. Even today a flock of sheep needs little shelter. Well-maintained enclosures and the watchful eyes of shepherd and dog will suffice.

Stout hog pens at a "progressive" farm in Iowa that dates from the early 20th century.

Early records show that the pig was one of the last farm animals to be enclosed. At home in the woods or munching away at the bracken avoided by all other animals, the pig required little maintenance. (The wild boar today is most often an escapee from domestication and behaves in a manner leaving no doubt that it prefers the forest and intends to stay there.) Its efficiency as a consumer then brought the pig inside its pen where it thrived on the waste from dairy and kitchen — thus becoming another animal that needed to be near the farm wife. It's easy to see why buildings began to cluster around the house.

Sparsely haired and bred for a life under protective branches, the pig did require some shade. It also needed the stoutest of shelters, since a hungry pig in its aggressive search for food could soon wreck a farmyard. Arthur Young, an 18th-century agriculturist, said, "In a large or even a middling farm, the hog is an animal of great consequence and proper places for keeping him must on no account be overlooked." He also asserted, "Nothing about a farm will make such quantities of excellent manure as hogs well-managed."

Chickens happily being given a free range in the barn. The problem is discovering where they lay their eggs.

The farmyard chicken flock, maintained to keep the family in eggs and provide meat for the dinner table, was kept to a manageable size. Chickens were easy to feed or able to fend for themselves, and there was plenty of shelter in the barn, stables, and other buildings on the farm, so that chicken coops were not an original farmyard priority. Coops, or hen houses, might be built only after other structures were in place, or when chickens or their eggs became a particular farm's product.

Handles on the posts allow the barrack roof to be raised and lowered.

Farmers looked forward to a good crop of hay each summer and would store it under any cover once the barn was full. Many seasons of overflowing barns led to the development of the hay barrack. It originated in Holland, and in turn led to the metal Dutch barn, which on today's landscape looks like an airplane hangar without walls. The original barrack, still common in the Netherlands, has a roof that can be raised or lowered for maximum cover and air circulation.

You will often see the silo, a uniquely American sight, on an abandoned farm, leaning against the barn. It is one of the newest shapes in this country's farm history, having been in use for only a hundred years. Silos are used to store fodder, or silage, usually made from chopped cornstalks, leaves, and cobs — valuable as feed if kept moist and away from sunlight. Large farms increasingly needed appropriate storage, leading to the appearance of the first square, upright silos in the Midwest. These first silos were inefficient; the corners created air pockets, causing the contents to spoil. Gradually they became hexagonal and finally evolved into the tall steel drums we see today. They were not popular in the Midwest at first, but the canny and more experienced farmers of New England and New York soon took to them and the silo then dispersed back to the Midwest. To me they are an alien shape. I know the silo is necessary and works well, but its industrial look is difficult for me to reconcile with the rest of the farmyard.

If you should ever entertain the notion of restoring a barn for other uses and using the silo as a spiral staircase tower to the hayloft, be warned that it's a waste of time. For these purposes, a silo is probably a farm's least useful structure. This huge, empty bin should be removed before it falls down.

The **windmill**, or wind pump, was the most conspicuous silhouette on the landscape before the turn of the century. Developed in the East, it was sorely needed on the Great Plains to gain access to underground water. Rotating at the top, the twenty-foot-high rosette would spin into the wind guided by the rudder, or vane, while producing a unique creaking sound. Some were counterbalanced with iron weights to make them stable in high winds. These weights often took the shape of horses, cows, and cockerels, or had celestial motifs. Such weathervanes are perfect examples of art at work, and have become highly prized.

The Homestead Act of 1862 gave settlers 160 acres of prairie land if they worked the parcel as a farm for five years. After the Civil War, thousands of veterans took advantage of the free offer, and the settlement of the West began in earnest. The acres given away by the government were principally in the Great Plains, an area stretching roughly from the Mississippi River to the Rocky Mountains. Although an immense and potentially productive territory, it was treeless, dry and covered with tough grass. Homesteaders survived drought, insects and loneliness, building crude sod houses to shield themselves from the extremes of bone-chilling cold in winter and searing heat in summer as well as from the relentless wind. The gusts were so strong and gritty that a standing joke became that if you wanted to sandpaper a board, all you had to do was hold it out in the wind for a few moments. Nature would do the rest.

Trees were few and far between, the pioneers fueled their stoves with dried buffalo and cow dung. They busted the sod with iron plows, and planted crops, and raised livestock. But water remained a pressing problem. Said one newcomer to the Plains, "This would be a fine country if we just had water." "Yes," replied a man who was heading back East, "so would hell." Rain was so scarce that a Nebraska farmer, when asked by a census taker when his teenage son had been born, answered simply, "That summer it rained."

By the 1880s, hardly a farm or ranch in the West was without a windmill. Some used a number of them. One ranch in the arid Texas Panhandle placed some five hundred windmills over its extensive ranges to water steers. Farmers who could not afford factory-made models constructed crude but relatively effective homemade ones. With a horizontal shaft added, windmills could be used for grinding, feed cutting and corn shelling.
From *Windmill Weights* by Milt Simpson, 1985

The vents for this New Jersey smokehouse are under the eaves . . .

. . . and a Tennessee tobacco smokehouse operates in the same way.

Smokehouses were extremely important

because the early farmers depended on the family pig for survival through the cold winter months. This always hungry but uncomplaining beast would eat almost anything and could put on weight rapidly — dependable food if it could be preserved.

Folk discovered long ago that pork was dangerous if not well cooked. They learned that a process of slow smoking over a wood fire would prevent the meat from spoiling, as well as improve the flavor. The building used for this process, the smokehouse, was usually a small shed not far from the farmhouse. And though hanging meat above the smoke from damp green wood seems simple enough, smoking was an art. Much time and patience would have been invested in a lone pig, and the farm family did not want anything to go wrong. The butchered pig was cut into sides of bacon and hams, salted, then hung from hooks above the earthen floor where the fire burned.

The flavor imparted from smoking came from the green wood on the fire. It might be anything but pine — apple, oak, and hickory were favored. Where trees were scarce, damp corncobs were used.

Here is some advice from Pennsylvania Dutch country: "It was important that the meat did not freeze while being smoked . . . since smoke does not penetrate frozen meat. Overheating with too much fire and not enough smoke is also very damaging. Too much heat causes the meat to become soft and may cause it to fall from the hook. [There may be] so much heat that the fat melts and is forced to the outside, the meat becomes partly fried and it becomes impossible to complete the smoking process . . . it cracks in most instances and becomes moldy, resulting in rancidness and spoilage."
From *The Pennsylvania German Family Farm*
by Amos Long, Jr.

There was just enough ventilation, usually under the eaves, for smoke to escape and to enable the fire to burn slowly. This was before the days of refrigeration: "Meats may be kept in it the year round, without being very much smoked, in as much as the smoking need be only occasionally renewed, so as to keep the flies away."
From *Barns, Sheds and Outbuildings*,
Byron D. Halsted, Editor

A working crib in Sussex County, Delaware.

The unique keystone shape of the corncrib as seen from the inside.

Today's combine harvester can bag wheat on the field. The grain is then trucked directly to the mill. Before this invention, the harvest was the farmstead treasure. Some farmers kept their grain in the farmhouse loft. This was risky not only because it attracted mice and rats but also because of the danger of fire from spontaneous combustion if the grain had not been thoroughly dried. Later there were grain bins in barns and still later railroads moved the grain quickly at harvest time. In the North and East, old granaries are recognizable by the short piers that serve to raise them off the damp ground. In addition, they were built with a double thickness of boards and no windows, to keep them tight and dry.

The **corncrib** was different. It was an American building that very much needed ventilation. It got its name from "cribbing" the interleaved logs at right angles to build up a structure, with the space in between providing ventilation. The farmer made the corncrib long and narrow, with the long side facing the wind to speed the drying of the corn. The famous inwardly tapering silhouette minimizes the amount of corn at the bottom, while keeping the heavier load at the top. When the small door opens at the bottom, the ears slide neatly out. Like granaries, corncribs were raised above ground, often standing on "mushrooms" that kept out rodents.

This local corncrib was turned into a childrens' playhouse.

Chickens peck away under a granary protected by 'mushrooms.'

A local privy in splendid isolation.

After a snowfall, a path was first shoveled to the privy or the woodshed, both conveniently near the house but most likely in opposite directions. In the 19th century, such a necessary building was barely described in guides to farm and outbuilding construction. This 1858 description can't bear to mention it by name.

"There is no building which is so generally located in the wrong place, as that diminutive house to which a name is applied that expresses the absolute importance of such a retreat. It is strange that a house which everyone is ashamed to be seen to enter, should be so often paraded in one of the most conspicuous positions that could be found, so that from all back windows of the dwelling house, it is the most apparent object in view. Probably there was once thought to be a necessity for this location of the building, arising from the idea that cleanliness required it to be placed at a considerable distance in the rear of the house. . . . The first improvement that was made upon the custom to which we have alluded, was to surround the front of the edifice with blinds, or with a trellis, behind which one might conceal himself before he made his entrance. The next improvement was to build a platform on which one might walk to it in muddy weather. At length it was

removed to the extreme end of the shed, and the unfortunate person who was obligated to retire to it might skulk around the shed, and allow it to be conjectured that he might have gone on some less ignoble errand. How ever much it might be suspected, there was no actual proof that he entered the temple that stood there; and a modest female after having occupied it without being seen to enter it, might on coming out return to the dwelling house with a feeling of comparative innocence."
From *The Farmers and Mechanics Practical Architect* by J.H. Hammond

You often can identify the site of an old privy — a lush apple tree or luxuriant evergreen standing as evidence of screening and enriched soil. The farm privy was not well built of stone or brick, even if other structures were, because it periodically had to be moved when the pit was emptied. Some were comfortable enough, but hardly a place for contemplation. Winter cold, summer insects, and built-in darkness saw to that. The familiar half-moon cutout on the door would provide a bit of light on the inside walls, which were usually whitewashed for purposes of hygiene and light reflection. Sometimes the family privy would be a wide two- or three-holer of various circumferences to suit different members of the family. Pungent herbs were planted around the outside, chosen more for their effectiveness against insects than for their welcome fragrance.

A late 19th-century three-holer in New Jersey.

Before indoor plumbing there were some attempts at efficiency. One arrangement, a bit more than a hole in the ground and a covered wooden seat, was the "earth closet" in which sand, lime, or ashes were very effectively applied to break down the contents of the pit. A frequent wash of lime was a good disinfectant. The Shakers designed trapdoors in the back of their outside closets and collected the chemically treated waste for fertilizer.

A stone-floored springhouse in Tennessee.

The purpose of the **springhouse**, built at the site of the fresh water source nearest the house, was to protect the purity of the family drinking water and provide a place to keep milk, butter, and other perishables. Most were built of wood, though stone or brick were best for a cool, even temperature. The floor of a good springhouse often was paved with stone and the walls whitewashed.

There is some money in old barn boards and timbers. The rustic look is very popular these days, and a Saturday morning visit to a large hardware emporium will even show you plastic versions of boards and timbers finished in barn red, complete with simulated grain. Old farm buildings are valued for their materials as well as for their history, and exposed timber is usually dry and free of rot and termites. Almost any old timber-framed building can be dismantled, starting at the top and reversing the order of the construction. If the timbers are marked, they can easily be stored for later reassembling. (My friends who save barns have six large ones stored inside one smaller one.) The decline and removal of a working building is a sad thing, and dismantling should be done only as a last resort, when there is no other means of preservation. Some who market barns piece by piece describe themselves as performing a public service. They promote the beauty of a tidied-up landscape, and see themselves as model recyclers and removers of firetraps. They usually sell to "designers" and decorators who create kitchens with a "country" look. Old farmers are wise to those who salivate over long, dusty, two-foot-wide boards and hand-made black-iron latches and hinges, but they also know that a farm is taxed on the number of buildings standing, not on their state of repair.

There are even building rustlers. A friend of mine who owns land on the New York/Vermont border discovered on a visit that the slates had been removed from a barn roof, leaving the unprotected frame ultimately to collapse. On a later visit, all the beams and posts were gone, with only sawdust left as evidence of theft.

A Vermont barn, about to move 200 miles south.

Barn posts, beams, and rafters neatly labeled and stacked.

The **root cellar** kept the family going throughout the winter. It was humid and cool, and stored food was kept below the frost line. The dirt floor and minimal ventilation maintained a constant temperature. When central heating, washing machines, bicycles, and other domestic overflow took over the old cellar, that was the end of one of its original purposes — food storage. When old farmhouses were built on rock shelves, root crops were stored in a separate cellar, usually in a slope nearby. These were mostly made of stone, with three sides built into the hill and the fourth side facing south. They were long as well as deep, with the contents held in place by the walls and separated by boards. Other root cellars were built as mounds on flatter ground, with steps leading down to the door. Anything stored was always below the frost line, of course.

Boundaries

Dry-stone walls at Pleasant Hill, Kentucky.

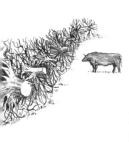

The most dramatic form of living history I have ever seen was an ancient root fence. I say "living" because those dense wood constructions take a long time to decompose — or burn. Black in the rain and bone white in the sun, these examples of concentrated energy are serious barriers, huge and hard, with their stumps as hubs. There is a measure of panic and desperation about them, like a circling of wagons, a fight against other forces of nature and the unknown. To organize the settlement of the New World, the calmer stone wall came along next, followed by the split-rail fence, the hedge, and even the sod wall when nothing else could be found.

A collapsed dry **stone wall** cannot be patched, as I have found from my own experience. One has to start all over from the ground up. The stone walls on our land, judging by trees, stumps, and old photos, were overgrown and logged out for generations. Thanks to the action of the hind feet of deer and the effectiveness of roots and brush, the discovery of our stone walls is often possible only after a light snowfall, when the silhouettes are at their best.

Although the early settlers were astonished when the right seeds took so little time to germinate and mature, they hated the stones, rocks, and boulders that had been tamped down by the primeval forest. While the farmer cursed, the patient oxen stood by, chained to the sled or stone boat they then pulled, loaded with rocks, to the planned edge of the field. There the rocks were laid, brick-like, high enough to stop a sheep or cow. As the next plot was cleared, another wall would be started parallel to the first. Any gap between the two was filled with enough earth and detritus to support the growth of a hedge. Alternately, the walls might be constructed from two parallel lines of stone built up from a wide base and filled with smaller stones and earth. Posts often were pounded into the gap to keep the more detemined rams away from the ewes; this was an adaptation

of the ancient Cornish hedge, where thorn bushes were planted in the gap. As land was cleared, even when stone walls were painstakingly laid up, an established tree would be left as a marker.

All good walls, like the Great Wall in China, are built wider at the base than at the top for increased stability. Other basic structures of architecture can be found in old walls, such as a very large stone placed across the wall — called a "through band" — that provided extra strength. If the stone was long enough, it might become a stile for the farmer.

A 'through band' in a dry-stone wall

The first stone walls in America did not have the permanence or look of labored perfection common in the Old World. The landscape was granite; the rocks were hard, but rounded and difficult to lay.

As settlers moved out and down from the glacial Northeast, limestone and sandstone were used for walls that resembled those on the British, Irish, and European landscape.

Walls were built of dry stone, without mortar. If not maintained, they would quickly give way to roots and hooves. One afternoon in Rhode Island, I saw a stone wall lose its ability to contain a flock of sheep. Spotting a dip in the wall, one ewe managed to get over it, dislodging a few stones. The flock followed, rear legs kicking backward as each one jumped, soon opening a gap six feet wide.

Walls laid by Shaker brothers in Canterbury, New Hampshire. The stones might be oddly shaped, but their facing is perfectly straight.

In heavily wooded country, settlers felled young trees and put up log **fences**. Soon after the first timber-framed houses were raised in new clearings, the trunks of young, straight trees were laid one on top of another to make simple fences. They went up in no time, their stability improved by occasional chocks. In time, thrifty farmers noticed that they could use half as much wood if they split the logs. This was the beginning of the rail fence. Up in the hills, rocks were either piled in the angle or against the rails. Evidence of this can still be found where the rails have long gone but signs of a wall remain, seemingly made by a drunkard. Snake fences were built with pride, but they took up a lot of land. At every turn in their crux a rail called a rider was laid. It was hard to knock down. My favorite was the Irish fence, never very popular but with a wonderful simplicity. Rails rest on the ground after passing through two pairs of crossed stakes.

A snake fence in the Blue Ridge Mountains.

The snake, or zigzag, fence was easy to build but required the most wood — split logs or saplings — because of the need to alternate direction to maintain stability. Stone or wood placed under the bottom rails prevented ground rot.

The buck fence was used on land too uneven to build any other kind. It is named after the sawbuck, a rack with X-shaped ends on which wood is laid for sawing by hand.

The stake-and-rider fence is simple to erect. A pair of crossed stakes, often pounded a few inches into the ground, provides support. A sturdy rail, the rider, rests in the cross. The lower part is made just like a rail fence

Also easy to construct, the Irish fence consists of a series of long poles or logs: the top end is placed in the crotch of crossed stakes that are wired or nailed together. The lower end passes under the two following crosses and rests on the ground

The fences seen here serve specific purposes. Neatly sawn board fencing encloses the house and barnyard. Tighter picket fencing protects the vegetable garden. More portable stake-and-rider fencing keeps animals out of the field crops.

An Irish fence strides across the meadow.

A snake fence with stakes and riders is a style used when timber was plentiful. This one is at Old Sturbridge Village, Massachusetts.

Eventually most land was enclosed by straight post-and-rail fencing. Although they look clean and economical, post-and-rail fences take work. They need deep post holes, require effort to make mortise holes in the posts, and the split rails have to be narrowed at each end to squeeze into the hole. Early post-and-rail fence builders had to look for rot-resistant cedar, locust, tamarack, or cypress; or, as a last resort, the bottom ends of posts could be treated with tar.

The invention of **barbed wire** barely caught up with the speed of America's westward movement. It was first seen as inhumane and too flimsy. Although invented in the East, it was extensively used first in the far West, then made its presence felt by moving back eastward, changing previously hedged or fenced land.

One of the worst or best of all inventions, we are still counting the costs and benefits of barbed wire. In a society that prides itself on freedom and independence, barbed wire is a symbol of the restriction of movement and still gives an alien look to the countryside. It is the stuff that wars are made of.

Still, barbed wire was extremely effective when used in the drift fences that ran for miles east and west over cattle ranches, stopping the inclination of herds to move down to the southern areas that were easily overgrazed.

In 1874, a year after Joseph Glidden's first patent, there were still only ten miles of barbed wire fencing. Ten years later there were 250,000 miles of it. Today there are millions of miles of barbed wire fencing in the U.S. alone. The look of the existing rural landscape is clearly connected to the western world's liking for beef.

Barbed wire from a fence put up more than forty years ago.

Neatly trimmed hedgerows seem to hold the land together.

Hedges, grown from seed, spread out to Missouri, to Iowa, Nebraska, South Dakota, and Oklahoma as people moved west in great numbers in the mid-1800s. The great forests of the East and North had thinned out and turned into treeless grassland except for the odd osage orange tree. A few new arrivals remembered the hedges of their homeland, wanted to encourage them, and on some wagons there was a sack full of osage orange seeds put up by enterprising sutlers in Illinois. In the desert regions, ingenious settlers made do with ocotillo cactus, which grew tall and thin and could be woven into wattlelike palisade fences. And the gulf states had the *Yucca gloriosa*, or Spanish bayonet, as an effective barrier. On the High Plains, where only grass would survive, hard work made sod fences from the very earth the plow turned over.

But America hadn't had enough time to allow hedges to grow as they did in Europe; if there had been, many of the later problems would not have occurred. In their favor, hedges were alive and they did not use valuable timber. Most importantly, they were good for the land, not just as windbreaks but in many other ways. They were the strongest stitches holding the patchwork quilt of fields together, valuable and worth re-establishing over here.

Hedges are the oldest barriers. When the Romans got to Northern Gaul and Britain they found these naturally growing but man-made barriers already in place. In our time, the soldiers after the D-Day landings found that hedges, or bocages, were a formidable obstacle for friend and foe. Established hedges have survived for hundreds of years, but in Europe have slowly but relentlessly disappeared in the name of farming efficiency.

In England, more than 115,000 miles of hedgerows have been removed in the last twelve years by developers and farmers who had invested in American equipment, designed for the prairie, that could not easily turn around on a typical European field.

Only now, after the cost has been added up, are the remaining hedgerows being left alone. They had been seen by some modern farmers as wasteful and untidy, and only needed to retain cattle in a world becoming more vegetarian. Hedges were a luxury, harbored pests, and hid precious sunlight from crops in adjacent fields; they had to be maintained and were no more than a historic feature.

An argument started when some traditional farmers and all the environmentalists wanted to keep the hedges. Earlier governments had urged farmers to grow more food crops and encouraged — even subsidized — them to remove hedges. Wildlife that had held farmland in balance began to disappear at an alarming rate. The hedges had for years helped to prevent pesticides from getting into the food chain. Aphids, a real pest for cereal growers, had been held in check by the birds and bugs nesting in the hedges. There was also a "hedge green," a permanent area left around the edge of the field so that machinery could turn. This "beetle bank," as old farmers called it, was never plowed.

Now that there is a growing public awareness of the benefits of restoring the balance of nature and retaining hedgerows, the wildlife that was almost destroyed by pesticides in the hedgeless country is coming back.

This is our **driveway**. It is very attractive, with a slight curve that rises and falls, flanked on both sides with meadow grass and post-and-rail fencing. It is our responsibility. The pleasing appearance of the driveway belies the fact it is not in good shape. The soft shoulders and ridge in the middle indicate that after years of use and much snowplowing, the surface has been pushed to the edges, becoming an unmowable home for wayside plants. You can see the exposed bedding stones in the furrows. Any gravel that was among them has mixed with silt and moved on down the hill, mostly into our stream.

It is a classic illustration of what happens over the years to a driveway that is on a slope, well-used, and frequently snowplowed. The driveway is our five-hundred-foot connection to the town dirt road. It can be repaired rather than rebuilt, not a big civil engineering job. It was built essentially the same way the Romans built their roads, with graduated levels of stones. I have to add big stones to those still there and lay them so that they curve down from the center. I'd then cover them with at least eight inches of coarse gravel and top off with a few inches of crushed stone, the expensive part that has disappeared into our stream.

Most important of all, the drive should always be higher than the ground alongside it — like a railroad on the prairie. This is even more important in the case of a sharply sloping driveway; without its crown, or camber, it will become a stream bed. We also need gutters on either side to channel heavy runoff. This has to be done before someone in a low-slung vehicle cracks an oil sump on the middle ridge or takes evasive action and starts making a new track to one side — and turns the whole thing into a mess.

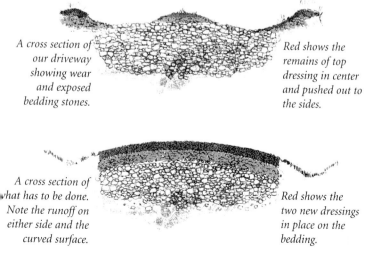

A cross section of our driveway showing wear and exposed bedding stones.

Red shows the remains of top dressing in center and pushed out to the sides.

A cross section of what has to be done. Note the runoff on either side and the curved surface.

Red shows the two new dressings in place on the bedding.

When we looked for a house to buy, one of the requirements was that the property include a pond or enough natural drainage to make one. Well, we have a good little pond and several spots for others. Our pond is three hundred and fifty paces from the house, a bit far for use in a domestic fire, but perfect for visiting wildlife and its own very active pond life. It rests on a shelf, a slight leveling out of a 1600-foot contour. The site was improved by digging and the raising of angled banks.

The area where we live, though very scenic, is officially described as ecologically fragile, its soil held intact by a dense cover of trees. The crust of heavy, acid clay covers an immense layer of glacial gravel, so that once the clay is dug the soil drains very well. The pond is spring fed, so we presume its location is natural. It is marvelously cold even on a very hot day.

I wanted the pond to be used as a home for a food source — trout, to be specific. It is about fifteen feet deep at its deepest, very likely the spot where the cold spring water rises. The temperature is just right for trout, but we have to restore the chemical balance with bags of limestone drawn up by sled in the winter and spread over the ice, ready for the thaw. The result of this effort is that the trout remain healthy and grow well. For the most part, the pond is well filled and maintains a proper flow. The runoff is screened to stop the fingerlings from joining the stream it feeds.

I have experienced only one problem during a rare, very hot summer, when a few fish died. I thought the lower depths and low temperature would keep the rainbows happy. However, an expert told me that the fish failed to find oxygen as they went farther down to escape the heat; there was none in the new water coming up from the spring. The trout had drowned in fifteen feet of cold, airless water. In the event of a repetition of such a problem, I've acquired a small air pump powered by electricity, with a hose long enough to reach the pond.

For the last sixteen years the pond has grown in maturity and appearance, which hints at a problem. The pond appears to be getting larger, but in fact its built-up banks, lined naturally with clay, are slowly sliding down and raising the water level. Eventually the pond will have to be drained and rebanked.

An experienced farmer described to a friend how a pond could ultimately disappear. "In the autumn the leaves from the trees on the hillside would cover the pond and then float to the banks on currents of wind. Then they would be composted by the topsoil and nutrients brought down by the streams and the rainfall. This humus and vegetation would build up until the pond became a swamp, and finally would end up as a meadow covered by topsoil."

A corner of our pond. 'You will no sooner have your pond dug than nature will begin to stock it.' — Henry David Thoreau

This sectional drawing shows what is happening to our pond. The parts marked in red show the gradual sliding down of the banks. The line marked in green shows the original banks and water level.

49

Animals

A working Clydesdale at an historic farm in England.

The horse was the backbone of the working farm in the 19th century, but by 1960 mechanization was almost complete. Since then there has been a small but steady increase in the number of working horses. There are several reasons for this: sentimentality, a feeling for history, and a genuine affection for the horse and the role it played in shaping the landscape. And though it seems that just about every possible farming machine has been invented, people still find tasks for a strong workhorse.

Much of the old farmland in our area has been naturally reforested, and logging is the main industry in the valleys. Ex-farmers learning about selective cutting are using Belgians and Clydesdales to harvest logs in the very hilly, often wet terrain that defies the ability of heavy, wide equipment to negotiate the narrow spaces between trees.

These big horses are descended from the Great Horse of Europe, which survived 400,000 years and four ice ages, roaming wild over the North German plains of Westphalia and the Rhineland. I remember seeing the last remaining herd several years ago, enclosed in a park near Paderborn, Germany. Their main descendants are the Belgian, Suffolk, Clydesdale, and Percheron, all originally bred as war horses to carry the weight of their own and their rider's armor, and later recruited into the work of pulling and plowing.

Today one can see these breeds at plowing contests and country fairs. Their groomed appearance and well-kept harnesses are typical — the plowman and wagoner have always taken great care of their teams and equipment.

The horse, originally hunted for meat, was so much a part of human life in France and Belgium before mechanization that it was considered a natural food source after its working days were over. During World War II the Continental Butcher Shops in every British town sold horse meat, the only meat that was not rationed. I could not bear to walk by them.

Traditions of the horse culture remain with us. Village garages and repair shops that were once smithies

Sister and brother Belgians in Washington County, New York.

remain in the same family. Everyday phrases demonstrate "horse sense": "taking off" derives from the act of removing the harness; "journey" from a day of work in the field; and "set you straight," is the saying of an experienced plowman guiding a novice and a team. Even a "train" was originally a line of forty or fifty horses tethered together, panniers laden.

Among the many breeds of horses developed, my favorite (perhaps because I saw it most as a child) is the Suffolk Punch — slightly smaller than a Clydesdale, a little darker than a Belgian, and without the typical feathering of long hair just above the hoofs. These shire horses are famous for their patience, manners, and willingness to work. They are known even to go down on their knees rather than give up on a pull. They could go on longer without a feedbag than most other horses.

George Ewart Evans spoke to a number of country horsemen, plowmen, and farmers before they passed on and before their sons became tractor drivers. The men were full of stories and ready to share their tricks of horse care and training. They swore by various mixtures of herbal leaves they rubbed on, or added to the feed, to make the animal's coats shine. They were competitive amongst themselves and with other farm workers, taking great delight in the mysterious ways by which they seemed to control, or even bewitch, their horses. Taking advantage of the horse's delicate sense of smell, for example, they carried strange potions they had mixed themselves to "jade," or stop, a horse dead in its tracks. To convince the locals of his animal's loyalty, one man surreptitiously dropped a "powder" near his untethered horse to transfix it outside an inn while he had a beer or two inside.

"One cunning old horseman used to jade a horse simply by pretending to feel the horse's fetlocks, but with the palm of his hand covered with the repellent substance. Later when he wanted to release him he had only to go through the same notion but this time having his hand covered with a substance that would neutralize the smell. And he gulled, and also impressed, the bystanders by lifting up one of the horse's front hoofs, giving it two or three sharp taps with his knuckles and saying confidently: 'Right! He'll go now.'"
From *The Crooked Scythe* by George Ewart Evans

Two Belgians in harness at a plowing demonstration in Hancock, Massachusetts.

Owners also could attract their horses with aromatic oils made from mixtures of herbs and spices rubbed on their own bodies, as long as they were upwind of the animals. So much for the current fashion for "horse whispering." And one must wonder at the "cure" used for the balky horse in the following anecdote:

"That night my father went out after it, but he did something before he left. As soon as he got to the loose box where they had the horse, he pulled a little bit of stick about six inches long out of his pocket and threw it right up into the manger. The horse went up to the manger and stood there. Then my father went in and put his headstall on and let him out. But he never did tell me what he'd put on that stick."
From *The Crooked Scythe*

The history of the farm horse is caught between the ox and the tractor, and working-horse lovers had their reasons ready for any debate about the virtues of one versus either of the others. Compared with oxen, a team of horses was more efficient since their intelligence allowed them to understand more commands. Sometimes a solitary horse would lead a team of oxen. Also, the horse had a longer working life and working day. And when the design of plows improved, it turned out that a team of two horses could pull better than six oxen. Machinery was invented with the horse in mind — mowers, rakes, and treadmills for threshing, for example. And finally, unlike an ox or mule, a horse can reproduce.

On the other hand, working with horses required more patience than that needed for oxen. The horse had to be harnessed, not simply yoked. Before that, there was rubbing down and currycombing. Harness leather had to be kept oiled and supple; the horse needed its shoes in good condition, and better food and shelter than an ox.

It's easy to see that the horse might be preferable to the ox. The choice between the horse and a tractor proved more difficult. The first tractors were priced to cost no more than a team of horses, and from then on the

A team being made ready for wagon pulling.

advantages of the tractor began to mount up. Even though the horse supplied manure from its fuel, the tractor was more powerful and could work longer hours. Therefore, in the end it was more practical.

Many farmers handled the transition to machinery with mixed feelings, since there was a real bond of affection between the working team of man and horse. But the plowman on a tractor still takes the same pride in his work, making a good furrow as he did when he walked over upturned clods behind the team, plowing and planting by feel and experience. Today he sits up high with a clear view ahead — but alone.

Think twice if you inherit a stable on your property, as we did, and are tempted to own a horse. A horse needs a great deal of care as well as a clean, dry, well-ventilated stable with a stall big enough to turn around in, and lots of exercise room. Rather than owning, you may want to offer to board a horse or two. The owners take overall responsibility for care of the beast, you have horses around to look at, and you'll get your meadow grass clipped and manured in the bargain. We did this once with a very old stallion. We were unprepared, however, for his ability to leap over fences when the wind blew the scent of mares toward him from the farm half a mile away.

I lost my city kid fear of big horses when, staying at a farm, I had to take a Clydesdale to the stable for harnessing. The horse knew where to go, but we had to cross some roads. I was being used to show that the horse wasn't lost. When we got to an open gateway I had an experience similar to that related in *The Crooked Scythe* by George Ewart Evans: "It is when they come into the fields with deep wheel-tracks, as deep nearly as half their little legs, it is turning into gate spaces where the children are obliged to cling to the horse's bridle and stumble along tip-toes, that the danger is." In my case, the rope tied to the bridle was very short and I remember hanging on and swinging as the horse lifted my ten-year-old weight over the foot-deep puddles.

SOME HORSE WISDOM

The man who does not love
a horse, cannot love a woman.

One white foot, buy a horse,
Two white feet, try a horse,
Three white feet, look well about him,
Four white feet, go away without him.

To protect a horse from witches,
tie a flint with a hole in it over the
stable door.

Dock a horse's tail so witches cannot
hold on to it.

Feed the horse nettle leaves for
stomach problems.

For worms, give the horse chopped
walnut leaves.

A mare in foal should never draw
a funeral wagon.

Rub a sweet-smelling substance
on a horse's forelock and
he will come forward.

A herd of Holsteins, with one Jersey for cream.

The **COW**, bred for generations as a multipurpose animal: a source of milk, cheese, beef, traction — even burden — and eventually leather and clothing, over time has been divided into three main groups. Paintings depicted milkers, in typical farm landscapes of England and America up to the end of the 19th century, as reddish-brown-and-white shorthorn or Ayrshire cows. Today most dairy farm herds are black-and-white Holsteins, bred to produce milk in great quantities. Part of the dairy group, often just one or two in a big Holstein herd, are the small and attractive golden Jerseys, known for their very rich cream. In the West (and elsewhere) white-faced red Herefords are raised to provide most of the world's beef. The third group is made up of crossbred animals, whose characteristics are continually being refined to adapt to living or market conditions. One of these is the Brown Swiss, originally prized as a puller, then for its meat, and now for its butterfat. Another is the white Charolais from France, increasing in numbers because it matures quickly and has meat low in fat. The type of cow bred into most others is the shorthorn. Recently the strain itself has been divided into the milking and the beef shorthorn. A further development in cattle breeding has produced cows that give birth to small calves, making delivery easier and less risky. Despite such specialization, not all the early original breeds have been nudged out of the farmyard, and

the cattle industry has begun to look at their virtues. In a recent test, for example, the British White, a breed dating from the Roman occupation, showed amazing potential. A young bull was randomly used in a test that compared it with animals chosen for their rapid growth rate: the best of the top beef bulls that year. The British White matched the competition for weight gain each day; and when it was examined for excess fat, it had less than any other bull in the test. Intrigued, the scientists carried out the experiment with other young British White bulls and proved that this ancient longhorn strain outperformed the modern breeds in weight gain.

Not all the old breeds can be maintained for experiments. As a result, they are under the same threat as are rare wild animals. Often, because they are not as photogenic as typical zoo animals, even petting zoos don't want them. But all is not lost. A famous zoo, in a cost-cutting move, began to feed its ancient livestock to the lions, saying that more space was needed for "wild" animals. Word got out, and Save the Tame Life groups were formed. Also, many of the growing number of "living history" farms have original breeds, and some new small farmers are finding out that small is beautiful when it comes to animals. Take the pretty Irish Dexter cow: she is half the size of a Holstein and gives half the milk — just right for today's family.

Cattle coaxing at Colonial Williamsburg.

If you stop to look at, or walk through, a herd of cows, their heads will turn toward you for a slow stare, then they'll resume grazing. Those that slowly walk toward you are probably heifers or bossies, still young and curious. They will stop when you stop, and you can gently shush them away. Sometimes there is a young bull amongst them. This is a prospect that frightens some youngsters but puts others in the mood for the excitement of the famous Running of the Bulls in Pamplona, Spain. Ferdinand usually ignores you — your red coat and all. But if he starts pawing the ground and backs away while facing you, then care is needed and the exits should be examined. The following action is not recommended but has worked. Here, the pitchfork becomes a symbolic banderilla:

"On one occasion Red Light got in with the herd of pedigree Guernsey cows . . . and there were panicky telephone calls from the family for me to go and remove him instantly. I went over armed with a pitchfork. I knew he would always try to back up to get a run at whoever was annoying him, so the only thing to do was to keep advancing on him with the pitchfork and he would keep drawing back. This he did, making nasty noises and digging holes with his feet to try to get enough room to charge, and I successfully backed him the three or four hundred yards to my own land. Colonel Miles was immensely impressed. I heard him telling his friends afterwards that I had fixed the bull with my eye and had forced him back, that it was great credit to my willpower and courage, etcetera, etcetera. In reality I was frightened out of my wits and knew perfectly well the only way to prevent him charging me was to keep walking forwards so that he would keep walking backwards."
From *Seventy Summers* by Tony Harman

The famous wild-looking Highland cattle.

Attractive Jersey cows, famous for their rich, creamy milk.

Sunlight turns this shorthorn into a rare breed. I was reminded that at the beginning of World War II, British bureaucrats instructed some farmers to paint cattle to prevent their being run over during the blackout.

SOME CATTLE WISDOM

Milkwort is said to increase the milk yield.

In Sommertime dailie, in Winter in frost,
If cattel lack drinke, they be utterly lost.

It is bad luck to step over a newly born calf.

Give a newborn calf a handful of salt to lick to ensure that it lives and becomes fruitful.

In rainy weather a cow has five mouths, for each foot destroys as much grass as it eats.

It is unlucky to put a lantern on the cowshed table — hang it from a hook.

When a cow is being served by a bull, make a small cut in her ear or nose to make sure she will conceive.

Have a billy goat or a donkey graze with the herd to prevent abortion.

Two young Brown Swiss oxen being raised and trained by a neighbor to work as a team.

The final eight lines from Maxine Kumin's "Watering Trough" evoke a bathtub placed in a field for the cattle to drink from:

*come slaver the scum of
timothy and clover
on the cast-iron lip that
our grandsires climbed over*

*and let there be always
green water for sipping
and muzzles may enter thoughtful
and rise dripping.*

A white Nubian doe.

The goat is the perfect animal for the full-time country resident but part-time farmer. It is ideal for the overgrown, neglected, small farm. I'll start with the disadvantages first. Goats need some shelter at night, which can be a converted old farm building. The goat is an eating machine bent on consuming anything in its path. To do that it will consume its collar (if any), the rope that tethered it, and the post that the rope is tied to as well. The word capricious is derived from the Latin *capris*, or goat, and some goats can be capricious. But as a source of milk, cheese, butter, chevon (fine-flavored meat), excellent manure, goatskin, and woollike mohair, it is a most functional animal — at least as far as humans are concerned. Male goats have a bad odor, but you wouldn't want a male anyway. Goats have to be securely tethered with a chain to a metal post, or fenced in with strong wire fencing at least six feet high — they can leap anything lower. The almost-invisible electric fence usually works, but when it fails the devastation a goat can do to your garden — or your neighbor's — must be seen to be believed. Despite all this, there are still considerable advantages to keeping a goat. Because goats are browsers and not grazers, they are not much interested in grass, yet mingle well in a field with sheep; they will eat everything the sheep won't. Although the goat should not be entirely used as a reaper, a pair of females would be very happy in a sheep meadow with occasional goat food as a supplement, and adequate water and shelter. I would advise owning more than one because goats are companionable herd animals, and a single goat quickly gets homesick and lonely.

All goats like company.

If you were to own two or three goats and regularly visit a registered local breeder, you would have a milk source for five or six years, and affectionate pets to follow you around, tails wagging.

There is work to owning a milker, though. For your daily gallon of milk, the doe must be milked twice a day. She needs grain, hay, and fresh water, along with her wild food from the meadow. Goat milk and cheese have been popular for some time now. The milk is highly valued because the fat particles are smaller and broken up, quite different from those in cow's milk; the cream takes longer to rise, making goat's milk easier than cow's milk to keep and freeze; and its components make it easier to digest, especially for children and those with digestive problems. Goat's milk makes wonderful, slightly salty butter, yogurt, and, of course, chevre, the soft, mild cheese so often used in cooking today's lighter fare.

All the breeds have their enthusiasts, but the Nubian, the Jersey of goats, and the smallest and most sweet-natured, would be a good choice for a new owner. (See the Bibliography for more information.)

A friend of ours who loves her herd of goats says that owning them is like boarding a group of teenaged girls. They are bright, up to tricks (and quick to learn all yours), and always want to sneak out, oblivious to the potential danger from dogs, and in many sections of the country, coyotes.

Nature's lawnmowers at rest in a parklike setting.

Sheep need little care, being placid outdoor animals. But American culture, for the moment, has passed the sheep by. Once supremely economical for wool and meat, the development of artificial fibers and changes in food preferences have drastically reduced the number of sheep in this country.

The great lawns of England were cropped by sheep. Grass regularly grazed this way is as fine as any in the world, with an even, manicured texture and few weeds except for wild thyme (which gives the meat flavor if the animals are butchered). Sheep need little water except in very dry country; they seem to get enough moisture from the grass. Only slightly less difficult to control than goats, they try to act like them, always looking for an opening in a fence; and sheep can jump almost as high as goats can. A determined ram will try to butt down what he can't jump over and can swim a river to get at ewes. The biggest problem — apart from predators — for anyone thinking of having a small flock of sheep is the handling of the wool each spring. Sheep shearing is difficult, and one has to find the whereabouts of a not-too-distant professional shearer.

There used to be a saying, "She's as common as mutton." It would now be taken as a compliment, for since 1970 the U.S. total of some 20,000,000 sheep has fallen to half that number and is still falling. Many Americans have never really been fond of the taste of lamb and mutton; in some areas one has a hard time finding top-quality lamb. The combination of beef, pork, and chicken leaves lamb with about 1 percent of the market. In fact, the prospect of government-supported lamb from New Zealand spurred the U.S. government to aid threatened U.S. farmers by taxing the imported meat, thus keeping its price level with the domestic variety. New Zealand does have one advantage, however — its spring lamb is born in August and arrives in time for Christmas. In the Old World, home-grown lamb is the first choice for Sunday dinner. French restauranteurs fly their buyers to Welsh meat markets to obtain the choice carcasses of lambs raised on salt-air grassland. Like the goat, the sheep was once a chosen source for milk and cheese — Roquefort, for example.

Regrettably, this hardy, low-maintenance animal is now a rare sight in the American landscape except in some parts of the West. Thousands and thousands of miles of overgrown stone walls in the eastern U.S. attest to the existence of the extensive wool industry of yesteryear. We are lucky that there is still no substitute for tweed.

This flock of long-haired hill sheep shows the mixing of breeds — Blackface, Derby, and Cheviot.

SOME SHEEP WISDOM

Once sheep have grazed a field, the next crop planted there will be a winner.

Wether: castrated male.
Teg: ewe having her first lambs.

Save the best hay for the lambing ewes.

Wethers fatten faster than rams.

Feed sheep a large amount of parsley to prevent foot rot.

Marking paint must be of a type that doesn't downgrade the wool.

Let lambs go unclipped, 'till June be half worne,
The better the fleeces will grow to be shorne.

You may begin to shear your sheep
When elder blossoms begin to peep.

The shearing pays the shepherd.

Leap year never brings a good sheep year.

Ewes yeerly by twinning rich masters do make,
The lamb of such twinners for breeders go take.

Unlike the goat, the sheep is happy enough in the cold and rain.

Each ewe will provide one hundred pounds of meat or eight pounds of wool.

One acre of meadow will support four sheep.

Many years ago, canny farmers buried their wool when they thought the price was going down. They knew it never rotted.

All dogs, unless properly trained, will chase and do great harm to sheep, which are no match for most dogs. Electric fencing seems to be effective at keeping unwanted dogs away. At the same time, no sizeable flock is complete without its sheep dog, and to see one of these animals at work is to see country life at its finest.

Tradition says the two black piglets at the front teat will grow to be the biggest of the litter.

Most domesticated **pigs** are descended from the wild pigs of southern China or the very wild European variety. Easily the most intelligent of farm animals, they can organize themselves into family groups and build nests of clean vegetation, depositing their dung and urine elsewhere. Life in the shade has given the pig a thick skin, but it is thinly haired and sensitive to sunlight, hence the sight of a pig wallowing like a hippo in the cooling mud on very hot days. But don't let this comical image fool you; hunters have found that the wild pig is violently aggressive in defending its territory.

Throughout history the domesticated pig has saved many poor families from devastating hunger, and nearly every medieval farm painting shows at least one.

When confined, the pig needed less room than other farm animals but could also be herded into the woods to grub up acorns or root around in the undergrowth. Peasants understood that everything they fed their pig would become flesh to keep them alive through the winter. The spring piglet might weigh as much as three hundred pounds by the time it was butchered in the fall. The smoked or pickled parts would last until spring.

A pig is a lot of animal, but its disadvantages are mostly superficial. It (like the male goat) has a repellent odor. Pigs don't jump but can knock down fences and posts with ease. Pigpens should be stoutly built of brick, with concrete or cobbled floors. Any lesser structure will need constant rebuilding. Pigs can even dig themselves out of enclosures.

Pigs are the most photogenic farm animals.

The simple advantages of the pig are these: rapid growth and large litters — a sow may have twenty piglets a year. In the past, the pig worked well in the dynamics of the farmyard, eating all the farmhouse food waste and thriving on the cast-off whey from the dairy. Furthermore, there was no need for a compost heap. When let into the orchard, pigs gobbled up the windfalls, often getting slightly drunk as the fruit fermented in their stomachs. During the war, when my family experienced acute food shortages, the local government issued special lidded garbage cans in which all the edible scraps were thrown in order to feed the pigs that would then feed us.

SOME PIG WISDOM
Baby pigs are very shy.

A starved pig is worse than none at all.

Pigs fatten well on meal of barley.

Pigs killed in the wane of the moon
will have inferior meat.

Unless your bacon you would mar
Kill not your pig without the R.

The first American pigs were brought
over to the West Indies by Columbus.

Rabbits are quiet and don't have an unpleasant odor, although their hutch will if it's not cleaned out regularly. During World War II and afterward, my family raised rabbits and chickens for food. The rabbits were easy to keep in a shady part of the backyard where there were a dozen hutches, barely containing the rabbits as they multiplied and grew. We survived the war with this backyard farming, which produced tons of manure fueled by dandelions, other weeds, the odd carrot, turnip greens, hay, and the same meal we fed the chickens. There was just one buck, kept quite separate except when needed, and each rabbit, usually in a stew, supplied us with more protein for its size than any other animal. I would not want to eat it every week as I did then, but I now regard a home-baked rabbit as a great delicacy. Like venison or mutton, rabbit flesh takes on the flavor of the animal's diet. The French country woman feeds her rabbits wild thyme, rosemary, and other herbs to raise them high on the gourmet list. I wish my family had known such secrets.

As a nine-year-old, I did not enjoy cleaning out the enormous number of pellet droppings in the rabbit hutch. But I did enjoy looking into the clean section where the doe would build a nest from her own fur in the semidarkness that all rabbits prefer. (We forget that they are nocturnal animals.)

Rabbits do make nice pets and are actually quite fastidious. And please remember that litters from one doe can yield up to eighty pounds of meat a year.

Rabbits and the Farmer

Rabbits are certainly not farmyard animals. Farmers have always disliked them as the cousins of the wild rabbit causing them misery, destruction, and in some cases, even bankruptcy.

Starting at six months old, a doe will have up to fifty kits a year that are ready for breeding at the same age. From mating to birth takes only one month. Out in the open, their burrowing that eroded fields, and their grass nibbling that took food out of the mouths of sheep and cows, was out of all proportion to the delicious benefits of an occasional rabbit pie.

In some parts of the world there were just too many rabbits. In Australia, a deadly virus was used to save the devastated wool farmers whose grasslands had been devoured by rabbits originally brought over from Europe. This concoction was so effective that when the rabbit threat was over, the years after broke all records for wheat, sheep, and cattle raising.

The rabbits died a slow, painful death. Some, however, were able to resist the virus, myxomatosis, and now the rabbit has made a comeback of sorts. But with the disease in their systems, the numbers never again will reach the millions there were before 1953. So far the farmers can live with this. It's just we cottage gardeners who are still at war with Fiver and Co.

Chickens are the only barnyard animals you can leave alone for an occasional weekend. They don't miss human company the way other farmyard pets do; they have a busy social life of their own. Their upkeep and management seems easier than that of rabbits or goats, but is actually more involved over the long term.

Chickens and other domestic poultry do not eat much leafy green vegetation; they need mostly protein and carbohydrates. The old farmyard had all this in plenty — weeds, insects, slugs, worms, seeds, and sometimes a handful of corn thrown from the back door.

Most small, spare buildings can be turned into a home for chickens, and in my experience most chicken coops are homemade. A hen needs only about three square feet of roosting or laying space, kept clean and ventilated.

Most naturally airy, uninsulated buildings are suitable for chickens, providing the roof is sound. The ideal coop should be about 10' x 10', but the adjoining run, if the chickens must be permanently enclosed, can be as big as you like. The coop interior should be whitewashed. (All you need to worry about is the chickens' flight ceiling of about six feet — and they don't usually want to fly even that high.) Such a space would suit a cockerel and his dozen hens, the normal social group. They will need perches their feet can grasp, clean straw for laying, and changes of water. Chickens are prone to disease in stuffy, confined areas. They discriminate little as to the whereabouts of their droppings. Let them out of their enclosure if space is available. This will make them "free range" chickens. Chickens won't wander far; they feel safe near the farmyard buildings.

A Rhode Island Red hen, just about to get the bug at the bottom right. The lettuce leaf on the left shows a near miss.

Serious gardeners don't want chickens anywhere near their vegetable rows because hens will peck away at the wrong type of green stuff; but with some common-sense fencing in the right places, non-laying hens will thrive on scattered seeds, hay, bugs, and grit, and get rid of their fleas with a nice dust bath.

The chicken farms that produced eggs and roasters for cities became an industry after World War II. In today's diet-conscious America, they have become principally a producer of white meat. (Good chefs will have nothing to do with America's factory-farmed chickens; they have their own suppliers.) There are no longer old-fashioned chicken farms; rather, there are controlled environments for the broiler industry. The supermarket chicken breast is from a well-fed, seven-week-old bird.

A controlled environment on the Delmarva Peninsula.

Eggs, unlike broilers, are no longer a growth industry. They also come from a similarly controlled environment, which in simple terms is operated by the light switch. In the country, hens lay more eggs as the days get longer because the longer day means more activity, more feeding, and therefore more eggs. So inside the plant the light stays on. It's an endless spring of fourteen-hour days of artificial sunlight.

Knowing that eggs and broilers come from the factory often inspires a collective nostalgia, and many folks have their country dream of owning a little flock of chickens. The hen that lays the best eggs will not be as tender as a non-broody one, we think, but both will taste a lot better than anything shrink-wrapped. And there is nothing like one's own *coq au vin*. (French farm people use the fresh blood to make the proper base for this delicious mixture from the farmyard, vegetable garden, and vineyard.)

But keep in mind that feeding laying chickens is not that simple — or inexpensive for that matter. A hen lays about two hundred eggs a year. She will need between-three and four ounces of good dry feed every day, and vegetables are needed in the diet as well.

Light Sussex hens getting some real sunlight.

SOME CHICKEN WISDOM

After a hen lays for two years, put her in the stewpot.

A hen should lay four eggs a week to be worth keeping.

If fed properly and kept clean, chickens will stay healthy.

When a chicken gets croup, give it leaves of rue.

Add chopped nettle leaves to chicken feed for good health.

Gather eggs once a day but be sure to leave the nest egg.

Monday is the best day to set a hen.

Never eat a hen mauled by a fox.

Burn dry herbs, juniper, or cedar to fumigate the hen house.

When a late-night visitor arrives for supper, and the poultry house is dark, grab the hen sleeping next to the cock; she is sure to be the fattest.

The chicken wire should go well into the ground. Foxes, coyotes, raccoons, opossums, and rats can burrow in, and even Rover, unless taught otherwise.

Chicken manure is the most powerful of all fertilizers. But the droppings on wood or concrete can dry like pigment on an oil painting.

"Crestfallen" comes from the time when the rooster's coxcomb droops from old age, inactivity, or threat from a younger, stronger bird.

Hens are good mothers and have frequently hatched orphan ducks and geese. As a non-swimmer she will go berserk if one of her charges heads towards the pond.

Chicken feathers make good dusters.

The bird is easier to pluck right after killing, before rigor mortis sets in, and will be tender and roast quickly.

For a week or two before killing, give poultry some barley mash mixed with skimmed milk.

The familiar white "Donald," or Long Island, duck came from China. It was the original Peking Duck.

The duck is a newcomer to domestication, but like the goose, it was always preferred in early America because it had more fat — and therefore better taste — than did chicken. After a duck has been roasted and the fat drained away from the meat, the flavor makes even the best chicken taste ordinary. Duck eggs are not popular because their flavor is pronounced and unpleasant to most consumers. The mass market prefers the tasteless chicken egg. Perhaps more important, the shells of duck eggs are more fragile than those of chickens and have less resistance to disease and transportation.

Ducks don't need as much shelter as do chickens and can manage without a pond unless predators are nearby. Female ducks are not very good mothers. Ducklings may follow mom everywhere because they don't trust her to be around when needed. If they are abandoned, a broody hen, if available, will look after them.

To protect his ducks from a persistent fox, a friend used a bend in the stream on his property to create an island. He then added a drawbridge, which was pulled up at night. A portable wire coop to protect newly hatched ducklings for their first few weeks was placed so that its solid end was a further deterrent.

Goose feathers were used for quills, and the down was gently plucked for filling pillows, a task that could take all day. If you do take on the job, keep away from any breeze and don't sneeze. The feathers will go everywhere and will take hours to settle down.

The look-alike goose and gander mate for life, as do swans. Ganders often fight amongst themselves.

Keep geese away from young trees; they will damage the bark.

One acre of grass is just about right for ten geese.

In the South, geese were let out into the cotton fields to eat the weeds. This was known as "goosing down."

Geese are easier to keep than chickens or ducks and are excellent and hardy "watchdogs." They can almost look after themselves, though a determined fox will go out of its way to seize a mother on the nest.

In the past, the goose was the original top-of-the-table bird, fit for the best occasions and, pound for pound, the most expensive. Everything about the goose was preferred: its taste, its lard, of course its liver. Its size made it just right for the whole family, even though it had nothing like the heft of today's domestic turkey.

Raising the Christmas goose gave country folk a way to anticipate a special occasion in their normally routine lives. The goose was happy through the spring and summer, fattening itself on grass. But at Michaelmas, when grass stopped growing and it had to be fed with grain, the connection with feasting began. The goose would be killed the week before Christmas and hung in preparation for its traditional roasting on Christmas Day.

Geese don't need a pond but do need a great deal of water. If allowed to wander they will turn your vegetable garden into a wasteland. They are incredibly messy; while they devour grass voraciously, their rich droppings will burn and kill their very food source.

The poor old turkey is a farmyard outcast. The domestic version is not quite sure what it is. The turkey is like a big, clumsy chicken, but needs bigger and better shelter, a more varied diet, and more extensive health care than its feathered cousins. And to top it off, like guinea fowl, they are incredibly noisy.

"They [turkeys] are amazingly stupid — from the newly hatched poults who can starve to death while trampling in their feed because they haven't learned where to find it, to the hens who lay their eggs standing up. . . . They are easily frightened. An acquaintance of mine who raised turkeys commercially went wild every Fourth of July because the fireworks in a nearby village invariably sent thousands of birds piling up in corners where they would suffocate unless he waded in and unpiled them. Airplanes going overhead had the same effect, and they didn't care much for thunder, either. And turkeys are much more susceptible to disease than other fowl are, especially if raised around chickens."
From *The Homesteader's Handbook to Raising Small Livestock* by Jerome D. Belanger

The plains that broke the plow. This is the still pristene Comertown Pothole prairie in Montana.

The boundless **prairie** was the first thing settlers encountered when they arrived at their measured sections to start a new life. The newcomer hitched up his plow and team, but the simple iron shovel plow just bounced in the tall grass, making no impression in the soil. The equipment was no match for a surface that had never been cultivated, with hard, thick roots reaching deep into the earth. Would-be farmers then teamed up, combined their horses, added weight to the plow, cut the grass and attacked the crust with axes and forced the seeds into the ground. Then John Deere made the steel plow in 1837, and his refined blade finally began to break the plains. The Native Americans had gathered their food among the grasses and saw the work of turning over the soil as a backward step, an upside-down method of growing. How right they turned out to be.

Millions of years of nature at work became undone. The simple sea of grass turned out to be a very complicated place; it was self-sustaining and didn't need anything.

Like birds, humans are primarily seed eaters, and it seemed a simple matter to get our daily bread from where tall grass grew. Wheat is a grass, but only works when cultivated. So plants that reseeded themselves were removed to make room for plants that grew seed for us as annuals. Gone were the grasses with powerful root systems that could defend themselves against drought, fire, frost, and wind.

A close-up of the well-maintained steel plow seen hard at work on the following page.

On the prairie there were 400,000 square miles of long grass to be used. Wheat, a sort of medium-size grass with puny roots, was planted there as if it belonged. But it needed protection of all kinds to survive. With such intensive activity, the land collapsed and turned into a dust bowl. The main lessons learned were that the prairie was now a fragile place and had been misunderstood. Farmers had to hold it together by strip cropping, contour plowing, and with windrows of trees. The land came back fast, but some lessons were forgotten. Farmers were encouraged to grow just one crop and get their own food from the supermarket. Back came the dust storm, which did not entirely remove the topsoil — it just deposited it somewhere else. Bare ground floods and erodes quickly. A lot of it found its way to the sea. The farming establishment's solution of cultivating less and adding weed killers was like an idea from the Pentagon. As Wes Jackson of the Land Institute said, "They poisoned the soil in order to save it."

The Land Institute has studied the prairie and is trying to prove that our food grasses can grow companionably with the original strongly rooted plants and life-giving legumes that ripen at different intervals, offering the potential of three harvests in one year from the same field. This kind of plan is worthy of a lot of lobbying, as it has a good gardener's approach to the future, creating a domestic prairie in which the original plants with their long genetic history can assist those planted by man to feed us and our livestock.

A prescribed burn being carried out on the Tallgrass Prairie Preserve, Oklahoma, just as nature would replenish it from a fire from lightning.

The look of successful **plowing** evokes the word "corduroy." Morning and evening light catches the furrows and illustrates the regularity of the pattern. When the crops grow, and right up until harvest time, the texture is further emphasized by rows increasingly soft and smooth. Stretches of log roads, called corduroy, were commonly laid across low, muddy areas before the age of asphalt. Country people liked the strength, softness, and warmth of corduroy in the winter over another hardworking cotton cloth — denim. In fact, farm workers identified with the pattern:

". . . the Doncaster Cord was in many ways the most interesting. It was woven to represent a field that had been horse-ploughed in the old narrow stetches. You'd have a band of ribs together to represent the furrows in a stetch; then a small gap to show the water-furrows between the stetches. Often times when I was going into the country after orders and so on in the autumn, I'd look at a field that had been freshly ploughed up after the harvest; and I'd think to myself how much like a piece of Doncaster Cord it was — colour, straight lines and everything."
From *The Crooked Scythe* by George Ewart Evans

The first long and narrow plowed fields required intense labor. The earliest plow was little more than a stick pushed into the earth at an angle as it was pulled through the soil, making a simple trench that would hold seeds. The wooden tool, called an "ard," was always under tremendous strain. There was great improvement when flint, and later iron, was attached to form a moldboard. Shaped roughly like an upside-down "L," it cut the soil both vertically and horizontally, turning the earth over and making a deeper, wider seedbed than the old stick-dragging method.

As a child, I remember that people who wore big, heavy boots had a nickname. They were called "clodhoppers," after the boots worn by the plowman who hopped to avoid the clods as heavy earth was turned. A crooked furrow often tripped up the novice plowman and made his job more difficult as his boots became heavily coated with clay.

Flexible birch branches harrow a plowed field at Old Sturbridge Village.

74

Plowing in spring and autumn calls for testing the soil first, mainly to determine its temperature. There are stories of plowmen not picking up the soil but sitting in it to test whether it was warm enough. They also would listen to the soil. If it made no noise — no crunching or squelching — it was ready for the plow. Before the days of artificial weed killers, some farmers chose to plant early to give their crops a head start before the weeds began to grow. Others waited until the first weeds appeared and then plowed, killing the weeds before they could do any damage. Some plowed their wheat fields east to west and then sowed north to south. This enabled the young shoots to get the most of the morning and evening sun.

Pride in good plowing continues today. A farmer likes to be known for his ability to build this basic architecture of the landscape. There are plowing demonstrations and competitions all over the country, not just with oxen and horses but with old steam engines and new tractors. The judges are hard to please. Straightness is confirmed by sticks placed at the ends of and along the furrow. Cuts must be vertical, and even more important, must be level. A stick is placed across the furrows; points are lost if it does not lie straight. Why does one need straight and level furrows? Proper furrows mean that later in the year the crops will come up at the same time and grow to the same height, giving the best yield. A plowman with a tractor today practices the same skills as his many predecessors: lining up on a distant tree, steeple, or silo; raising and lowering the plow he pulls to accommodate the changes in terrain. I did see one farmer get his tractor to work like a horse, by putting it in gear with two of the wheels on one side well furrowed and walking just behind it, just stretching his legs.

The sound of the tractor has now drowned out the jingle of harnesses and the chink of stones hitting the plowshare, but the task and the result have not changed a great deal. The patterns are the same, the last row is still done to face the gate, the way the plowman came in. What is different now is that most hedges, walls, and fences have vanished.

Below I have sketched two methods reccommended to small farmers using the first tractors.

The alternating system plowed the equivalent of two rows at every turn.

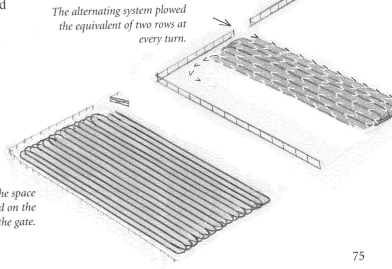

The zigzag system leaves the space for one continuous row to be plowed on the return journey to the gate.

75

The versatile M Series Farmall.

The backyard horse, used for pleasure, is a familiar sight on small farms throughout the U.S. even though the area it requires — to say nothing of the cost of its upkeep — may be more profitably devoted to other purposes.

"Even the work horse is open to the objection that though he may be a good worker there is not enough work to keep him busy a sufficiently large proportion of the time, he must be fed, groomed, bedded and watered almost as diligently while idle as when at work and given time-consuming exercise in order to keep him in good health. So far as the small farm is concerned heavy work such as plowing may be done more economically with a rented team or a tractor or even by a hired plowman or tractor owner."
From *Five Acres and Independence, A Handbook for Small Farm Management* by M.G. Kains

Today the **tractor** is part of the farmyard landscape, both physical and mental. As the growing and nurturing instinct comes out in many women who move to the country, the urge to mark turf, to patrol, to attempt to improve the landscape comes out in many men. The urge for a real "hands-on" experience makes some men even dream about owning a tractor. I probably don't need one, for example, but I have not yet given up trying to convince my wife that, with a tractor, the lumberjack in me could haul my chain-sawed wood to the woodpile, pull a big brush hog to keep the weeds down, plow us out of a three-foot snowfall, and get up and down our hill when the road is impassable. Actually, the sensible thing is to hire someone to do all this or ask a neighbor who has a tractor — which is what I've done. However, I have learned a few things about tractors along the way.

Tractors are very reliable once you get them going, but like horses, they won't function if not used regularly.

The original steam traction engines did not move once they were in the field. They were the power source that activated the belt-driven threshers and binders.

An old Allis-Chalmers gets a new — and slightly different — coat of orange paint. Originally, tractors were painted dark reds and greens, similar to steam locomotives — not the nursery colors of today's John Deeres and Fords.

A well-looked-after general-purpose tractor demonstrates its belt-driving power. It was driving a 1940s' harvester on the other side of a ditch.

Farmers know a lot about tractors because they've had to fix them on site — auto repair shops do not handle tractors, and maintenance centers are a long way from the field or farmyard. The difficult terrain in our own area means that most farmers even have their own welding apparatus.

There are basically two types of tractor: general purpose and utility. Most people make do with the utility version unless heavy plowing is to be done. With its low center of gravity and power takeoff on the rear axle, the utility tractor is an efficient means of pulling attached implements such as mowers and rakes; it can also be used for the odd log-splitting job or even to run a home sawmill. The most familiar old tractors seen on small farms are the Ford N series and the famous red Farmall with its tricycle-style wheel arrangement. Although this latter makes for easier maneuvering in tight spaces, there is some loss of stability. Unlike cars, tractors are adjustable and much lower geared with slower rpm, so that twenty horsepower is power enough. Many have diesel engines — famously hard to start on cold mornings but stronger, heavier, and less complicated than the gasoline variety. A trusty old diesel needs a good battery in the winter for the hard work needed to get the pistons moving.

The general-purpose tractor is usually bigger, with a higher clearance, and is more sophisticated than the utility type. The working parts are set within the frame so that attachments can operate beneath as well as behind the tractor. Sometimes the engines are mounted to one side so that the driver can look down at an implement while it does its job.

Having said all this about tractors, a four-wheel-drive, all-terrain vehicle with a towing hitch would do just as well if all you want to do is pull in-the-way tree limbs from one place to another.

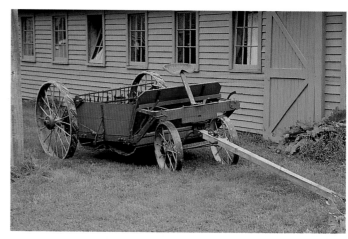

Spreading lime at Hancock Shaker Village.

The spreader cleaned up, Shaker style.

A horse-pulled disc harrow with rocks supplementing the driver's weight. By this adjustment, he could adapt to the condition of the soil.

This still-working reaper-binder looks as if it has been dropped from above. The revolving sails push the wheat into the path of the cutter.

Some local farmers gain great pleasure from occasionally using and demonstrating the old methods.

For the lay reader or *arriviste* to the countryside, the best way to understand the huge machinery poking out of sheds or abandoned on fields is to read Verlyn Klinkenborg's *Making Hay.*

In it he describes exactly what binders, threshers, windrowers, and combines do, how they do it, and what it feels like to work with as well as watch farmers and machines at their business.

Growing your own

I think I'm a terrible gardener, but I'm beginning to enjoy it more. Since moving to the country I have raised our produce. I imagine my gardening has been heavily influenced by my childhood experiences in the backyard when I worked with my grandfather in his garden, or allotment, or shirked when asked to help my father or the neighbors. The British seem to enjoy the challenge of gardening: the possibility of beating the odds; growing plants in Britain from far-flung countries of a past empire; gardening in a climate that means working in the damp and drizzle.

The "temperate" British climate may, in the long run, be best of all for growing, but it's the long run that I remember more than the results. It was when I moved to upstate New York that I saw the difference. A few days after sowing, the seedlings came up with what I thought was astonishing speed. This was very encouraging. I had been used to watching and waiting, covering the plantings with cloches, praying for sun, and pulling up weeds that appeared well before the pale green dots of lettuce.

The wisdom collected on the next few pages, learned from personal experience, is mostly for the first-time gardener and is almost entirely about food, or plants that add to its flavor. I am not interested in cultivating flowers except when they are edible. (I do like to have them around, and when our fields are ablaze with wildflowers, walking our path through them is a favorite pleasure — with no work necessary.) My wife thinks otherwise. She grows flowers with various scents and bright colors. They would look good in our fields, too. It's just flower beds I don't like. They evoke suburbia and parks with "Keep Off" signs. My wife says my view of gardening is really all about the war and survival.

Two flowers I like— the amazing flower of the artichoke and the bug-scaring marigold.

Why grow vegetables, anyway? Supermarket produce is cheap, and with refrigeration and shipping as well as greenhouses and advances in plant genetics, practically independent of season. In most places there are also local farm stands and markets. It is my opinion that gardening should be the country newcomer's first activity. It's the opportunity to meet nature at the halfway point. Gardening, just like farming, can be arduous, but at least a decision as to the size of the garden can be made according to one's own capabilities.

Gardening is creative labor, and unlike factory or office work, one gets to see the product all the time. Gardening is also work that can keep us alive. Our bodies are designed for bending, digging, planting, and picking. The technology-minded Shakers, for example, knew this, and for a long time the hands of their many garden workers won against the machine.

Gardening tools are simple and have evolved over many generations. They are forgiving to use, too, and take left-handed people into account more than most other gadgets. (I noticed, when I studied their gardening methods, that the gardening forks, spades, and hoes the Shakers used were longer than most others and easier on the back.)

A Shaker spade.

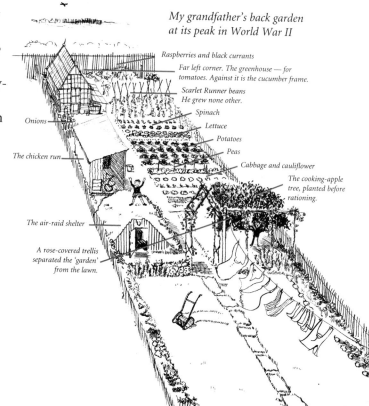

My grandfather's back garden at its peak in World War II

Raspberries and black currants

Far left corner. The greenhouse — for tomatoes. Against it is the cucumber frame.

Scarlet Runner beans
He grew none other.

Spinach

Onions

Lettuce

Potatoes

The chicken run

Peas

Cabbage and cauliflower

The cooking-apple tree, planted before rationing.

The air-raid shelter

A rose-covered trellis separated the 'garden' from the lawn.

The vegetable **garden** is like a farm in miniature. The plot has to be plowed or dug, fertilized, weeded, and harvested in the same farming year. The beds can be seen as fields with crops that do, or don't do well next to each other. Parts to be left fallow or rotated, and conditions in surrounding planted areas, whether good or bad, will also have an effect.

Even before you start to think about the vegetable plot, it is a good idea to have something growing by the kitchen door, cherry tomatoes in pots, or herbs, for example. They will benefit from the shelter of the house and probably do better than in a more exposed site. From there you can choose the place for the garden. There is usually one good spot, and it has been used before.

Today, though, aesthetics have become increasingly important. New arrivals to the country have often moved the garden patch away, preferring a flower-edged lawn, and have paid the consequence. Tucking a garden away from sight, even when fenced, invites unwelcome visitors. The farming people where I live put their plots in the middle of a big open area near the house.

This is usually effective, and there is no need for fencing. The critters, rodents, deer, and birds prefer cover — to come from, or run to when discovered — and avoid open spots instinctively. They know the distance they need to get out of trouble. An open plan makes digging, tilling, and altering the size of the garden much easier as well.

The first mistakes we all make, no matter what the packet says, are to plant and grow seeds too close together and to grow too much. I have found from experience that there is no safety in plant numbers and that reducing the number of plants by thinning will, in the end, produce a bigger and better crop. I'm still amazed at the quantities of vegetables this climate can produce compared with that of most of northern Europe. I grow squash and cucumbers near a fence because eventually I have to throw a lot of them over it.

The first garden is often a success, but it is difficult to repeat that success the following year. One reason is that the weeds that had been choked out by established grasses will return more strongly on the disturbed ground in the second year. Most first garden plots benefit from long dormancy. They are full of natural nutrients, well-balanced, and fresh to the spade. An undug meadow is less compacted, "breathes" well, and has found its equilibrium. Sir Albert Howard, the pioneer of organic gardening, saw that topsoil contained more air than its subsoil, enabling organisms to release food to plants naturally. Also, organic matter reproduces itself. Howard dedicated his life to proving that the raw material was the most important factor in organic gardening and that the way to bigger yields was to bring air and organic matter together in the soil, mixing it and making the soil lighter. He argued forcefully against tradition, insisting that artificial nitrates and phosphates were unnecessary and that nature did the job better. Today the word "organic" is everywhere, but we can ruin Sir Albert's work easily, obliterating valuable topsoil by digging too deeply and turning the airless, nearly dead subsoil to the surface.

Digging your own garden is the way to discover its secrets. Wear gardening gloves or be prepared for blisters. My first big digging experience was to earn pocket money as a ten-year-old. My task was to "turn over" a heavily overgrown 50' x 50' plot with a garden fork. I had to dig down and come up with a large, grass-covered clod, shake it, break it up, and throw the top and its roots onto a pile. I was to continue this until I had tilled the whole garden. After half an hour, palms already blistered, I had had enough. The earth seemed to be solid, wet clay, drilled with long dandelion roots, and the clods — when I could lift the fork — stuck to the tines like glue.

I was screened by a solid wall from the neighbor who was exploiting me for the equivalent of twenty-five cents, so I began to dig down and just turn over the earth,

effectively covering up the surface green. The air began to dry the exposed soil. In my determination to finish the job (or to make it look like I had), I actually improved it. My customer took a look, threw some lime over it, and seemed well-pleased. He could find all the roots later. But what I did turned out fine. Organic matter had been dug into the soil. It decomposed in time for the spring planting.

Michael Pollan's *Second Nature* is the perfect book for anyone thinking about starting a garden for the first time. It is about how a garden can fit into the wild and how we can be reconciled to it (after a few battles). It is worth reading for the chapter on weeds alone. As Pollan learned, weeds are us, and the distinction between weeds and American wildflowers is yours to decide.

Most of the weeds that plagued the European gardener came to America as stowaways. Daisies, St.-John's-wort, crabgrass, clover, timothy, buttercups, Queen Anne's lace, groundsel, lamb's-quarters, chickweed, and more came over in domestic animals' manure, in the earth used as shipboard ballast, mixed in with grain, even affixed to soles of boots. Dandelions were brought over for salads, plantain roots to make flour. Even tumbleweed arrived accidentally from the Ukraine as settlers from that far country reached the High Plains. These imported seeds could wait patiently, for years if necessary, for the one thing they needed to thrive — plowed ground. I have become increasingly interested in learning which of these weeds are edible, not just dandelions for their young salad leaves and violets to accompany the peppery nasturtium flowers, but burdock, jewelweed, lamb's-quarters, sheep sorrel, and many other invaders. The more we eat them the more they'll disappear — perhaps.

So here are a few lessons I've learned about (relatively) painless gardening. First read about the soil itself, then the plants, their fruit and what can be done with them, and some gardening wisdom. Later we will all be ready for leeks, celery, and the pursuit of asparagus.

The delicate-looking yellow sorrel below usually comes up in the spots where my wife grows her salad nasturtiums. It has a nice lemon flavor.

Your garden soil needs a balanced diet if it is to remain — or become — healthy. Don't treat your soil like dirt. Kits available at garden stores allow you to test the amount of soil acidity or alkalinity (pH) and then adjust its composition for your growing purposes.

Topsoil is the loose layer of earth that supplies plants with the nutrition they need to grow and develop roots. In order to have soil with a good texture for growing, you need to concern yourself with its main ingredients — sand, clay, and humus.

Sand, composed of large and loose particles, makes for a light and easily worked soil but one with no food value. Soil with too much sand will dry out quickly and needs feeding with organic matter to help bind soil particles and hold water.

Clay is a tightly bound mass of tiny particles. Soil with too much clay, called "heavy" soil, holds water and obstructs the passage of air. When dried out, clay soil can become as hard as a brick. Clay, however, is chemically active and provides plant food; therefore, the ideal is to have clay and sand in proper proportion.

Humus, which is decomposed organic matter, also serves as a storehouse of the nutrients needed for successful plant growth. Thus, it is important to build up the soil's humus content. In addition to the nutrients provided, the microorganisms in decomposing humus help protect plants from diseases and insects.

Depending on varying conditions and needs, there are other substances a gardener can add to help correct imbalances or make soil richer; they include manure, compost, green manure, leaf mold, seaweed, wood ash, and lime.

Manure usually means animal dung, and the best comes from cows, horses, and pigs. Cow manure obtained from winter feeding is preferable because it does not carry the weed seeds or insect pests as does manure from pasture feeding. Horse manure is very rich because the animal's diet includes a large amount of grains high in plant nutrients. (Fresh animal manure should be composted, not applied to the garden immediately.) In addition, poultry manure is considered of great value if it is mixed into the compost heap. If getting and curing fresh manure is too difficult, bags of composted manure are available at your local plant nursery.

Three-stage compost bins.

The compost pile refers to the place where vegetable materials decay and, through the generation of heat, turn into humus. When decomposed, the material will be black-brown, slightly moist, and will bear no trace of the original grass, eggshells, vegetable peels, etc. Properly made compost actually smells sweet, like a walk in the woods.

The best way to compost organic matter into humus is to start with a good container. The optimum height is around four feet — high enough to maintain necessary heat but not so high that matter is packed down too much. A three-stage bin with removable sides makes it easy to turn the compost and also provides an ongoing supply of humus. Graded bin size allows the maturing compost to be turned into the next smaller bin as it shrinks, and a new pile to be started in the largest one.

Green manure, often called a "cover crop," is the rye, alfalfa, or clover planted after the harvest and later tilled back into the ground. This crop supplies the soil with nutritional organic material. Green manures are perfect for gardeners who cannot compost enough material for larger areas.

Leaf mold from deciduous trees is a valuable source of humus, which lightens heavy soils and helps light soils retain moisture. Leaves are shredded to help speed their breakdown and then placed in a fenced- or wired-off area until ready for spreading on the garden. Nitrogen in the form of manure or dried blood often is added to the pile because the leaves alone do not contain enough nitrogen to feed bacteria. It may take several years to get the same fine black mold found on the forest floor.

Seaweed, one of the oldest manures known, is very rich in potash, which is beneficial to the growth of potatoes, beets, and cabbage. It also is effective because it is free from weed seeds, insect eggs, and plant diseases. Small amounts can be used to "heat up" the compost pile and accelerate breakdown, especially if first soaked in hot water. Commercial extracts also are readily available to the gardener.

Wood ash from a hardwood-burning fireplace is a source of potash. It should be stored in a dry place and mixed with other fertilizers, or spread directly on the ground at least a few inches from plant stems. When rain falls, its nutrients are leached out and absorbed by the plants. (Wood ash is especially good for tomatoes and onions.)

Lime often is needed to make the garden more alkaline. This is especially true in areas where there is no naturally occurring limestone and the soil is therefore too acid for most vegetables. Ground limestone is recommended because it breaks down slowly and is available to plants over a long period. Lime should not be used at the same time as animal manure because it causes the loss of nitrogen. Adding manure in the fall and lime in the spring keeps them well apart.

This year, as I write, our vegetable garden has been very successful. We have now learned from experience that we can have an autumn crop of peas and that we should never bother with arugula until the end of summer. (Our craving for it resulted in it bolting through the spring and midsummer.) Each year there is something new in the garden, and in the case of heirlooms, something old. I do not resist the temptation to grow the easy ones, but have given up on plants that I tried to like because they were good for me, such as radicchio and chicory.

A well-designed vegetable garden with plenty of space between rows.

The Spanish conquerors brought **tomatoes** back from Peru or the lower Andes, their place of origin, to Spain in the 16th century. These tomatoes, described in writings of the time as being small — somewhat larger than a cherry — and yellow, became known as "golden apple" or *pomo d'oro*.

Many cultivars known today are derived from this same wild species. Although the tomato was soon planted in gardens in southern France, Italy, and England, it was grown primarily as an ornamental plant for almost two hundred years before its culinary use became widely accepted.

This is 'Ronclave,' *a tall-growing indoor and outdoor tomato.*

'Gardener's Delight,' *a cherry tomato from Britain. Slightly larger and more acid than the* 'Sweet 100'.

The easy-to-grow and reliable 'Sweet 100' *brings back the flavor and sweetness of yesteryear.*

The ornamental tomato, brought over to Europe as a decorative plant.

The plum tomato, developed for the consistency of its flesh, is useful for sauces. This is 'Plumito

The hardy heirloom 'Tigerella.' *Wonderful in salads.*

Red Robin,' *the smallest of the cherries.*

Two heirlooms. The smallest, 'Yellow Currant,' *resembles the original* 'Pomo d'oro' *brought to Europe early in the 16th century. Next to it is the* 'Cherokee Purple,' *a native from Tennessee.*

A spider feeds on a bug among our young Beefsteaks.

I use cages for small 'Gardener's Delights' only. Big fruit bruises easily.

Thomas Jefferson was one of the first to raise tomatoes in this country, and his writings note that they were planted extensively in Virginia by 1782. Indeed, tomato recipes are included in Mary Randolph's *The Virginia Housewife* (1824) as well as Eliza Leslie's *Directions for Home Cookery* (1828). When tomatoes became part of American cuisine, they were always eaten well cooked in catsup, sauces, soups, and side dishes, or were pickled.

Botanically the tomato is a fruit, although legally it is a vegetable in the United States. (The Supreme Court ruled in 1893 that since it was used as a vegetable it should be considered one for the purposes of trade!)

Often, on the way home from school in early autumn, I recall our gang purloining a few ripe tomatoes growing near a neighbor's fence. We would bite into them and suck out the mixture of juice and pips, chucking the rest away. We felt that the juice was where the flavor came from. In recent years I have never been able to understand recipes that command the cook to do away with my favorite part of the tomato.

Agribusiness has developed tomatoes that are basically tasteless but have tough skins and are thus suitable for shipping long distances. As a backlash to the work of big growers, there is now a movement among local farmers and private gardeners to plant heirloom varieties. Heirloom tomatoes, with their various colors, shapes, and intense flavors are rewarding to grow — even if they don't always look as pretty as those developed by the agricultural business experts. Seeds are available through gardening catalogues, and heirlooms noted there recently include: 'Cherokee,' 'White Wonder,' 'Gardener's Delight,'

The smallest and the sweetest.
Clockwise, here are 'Gardener's Delight,'
'Tigerella,' 'Yellow Canary' *(two bunches),*
'Yellow Perfection,' *and mixed ornamentals.*

'Persimmon,' 'Big Rainbow,' 'Brandywine,' 'Costaluto Genovese,' 'Evergreen,' 'Green Zebra,' 'Purple San Marzano,' 'Principe Borghese,' 'Arkansas Traveler,' 'Zapotec Pleated,' 'Yellow Perfection,' 'Red Currant,' and 'Yellow Pear.'

Start your own tomatoes indoors from seeds, or buy plants at a local nursery, which generally will carry varieties that grow best in the area. Often such nurseries will be willing to start special or heirloom seeds in their greenhouses if you discuss it with them in advance. The owners of our local nursery always encourage us to try the heirloom varieties they grow, and welcome the feedback from our experience.

Tomatoes are easy to grow if they have a sunny, well-drained spot in the garden and if the soil is prepared. Dig the soil and work in compost or decomposed manure to

enrich it, since tomatoes are heavy feeders. If your soil contains a large percentage of clay, add sand and peat moss to lighten its texture. Tomatoes like soil with a pH of 6 to 6.8.

Drive sturdy, five-foot stakes into the ground next to each planting hole. As the plant grows, tie the main stem to the stake with soft twine or yarn. Be sure to set out the plants after all danger of frost has passed and cover the ground with a thick mulch to keep the soil moist and inhibit weeds. Fertilize about once a month. Good growing companions for tomatoes are onions, parsley, and carrots; bad ones are the *Brassica* family, corn, and potatoes.

To keep the plants from putting too much energy into leaf growth, pinch out side shoots when they are small. These "suckers" grow between the main stem and the leaf stem.

This recipe requires a food mill, which eliminates the time-consuming and messy task of peeling the tomatoes.

6 quarts of quartered tomatoes
6 carrots, peeled and quartered
6 garlic cloves, peeled and halved
3 cups onions, chopped
1 cup fresh basil leaves
1 cup fresh Italian parsley leaves
kosher salt to taste

1. Rinse tomatoes, cut out stems and any bad spots. Quarter, measure, and place in a large, heavy-bottomed stainless steel or enameled pot.
2. Add carrots, garlic, salt, and onions.
3. Cook over low heat. After enough juice has been released so the bottom of the pot will not burn, increase the heat and bring to a boil.
4. Add basil and parsley. Lower heat, and simmer for 2 hours, stirring occasionally. Remove from heat and cool.
5. Place a food mill, fitted with the disk with the smallest holes, over a large bowl and pass the mixture through, a little at a time. The pulp will go though, but the skin and most seeds will not.
6. Transfer sauce to pint-size plastic containers. Store in the freezer.

Yield: 6 pints

When the vines are loaded with tomatoes (more than one can possibly eat), there are three fairly simple ways to put some away for the winter. If there is ample room in the freezer, cherry and other small tomatoes can be frozen whole on a tray and then sealed in plastic bags. Saved this way, they can be dropped straight into soups, stews, chili, etc., and have all the flavor of fresh ones. (Note: They turn mushy when thawed.) Tomatoes can be dried either by using a dehydrator or the oven. In both cases, make sure the tomatoes are ripe but not overly soft. Rinse, dry, core, then cut plum types in half or quarters, round tomatoes into thick slices. Place cut side up on drying racks and salt lightly. Follow instructions for the dehydrator, or place tomatoes in the oven at 140°F and dry until leathery. This will take from five to eight hours, depending on the oven and the thickness of the pieces. Check often near the end of the time suggested. Cool completely and store in clean, dry quart jars. If you prefer, you also can cover dried tomatoes with olive oil.

For a basic, all-purpose sauce that can be turned into soups or more complex sauces, see the recipe at right.

'Gold Crest,' *ready in 67 days*

'Kelvedon Sweetheart'

'Sugar Daddy'

'Miracle'

'Indian Dawn'

'Mellogold,' *ready in 82 days*

'Earlibelle,' *ready in 71 days.*

'Green Midget' *has very short cobs.*

'Eclipse'

Corn, also known as maize, is believed to have originated in Central America and the adjoining area of Mexico, where it has been cultivated for thousands of years. It sustained the cultures of the Aztecs, the Mayans, and the Incas. Corn slowly moved north and became a staple crop wherever it was planted. As we were told in our early history lessons, Indian corn saved Captain John Smith and his party from starvation in what is now Virginia. Farther north the Indians showed the Pilgrims how to plant corn in hills and fertilize it with fish.

Country gardeners like to joke about planting corn next to a fence. The night before it's time to pick those perfect, sweet ears, raccoons will climb in and have a feast. And, if the fence is too high, a few deer will show up so the raccoons can jump from their backs into the garden and throw ears over the fence for all the animals.

Sweet corn can be grown with relative ease in most parts of the country, but it is a heavy feeder and will deplete the soil unless rotated every year. Purists take it straight from the garden to a pot of boiling water, but it's almost as good to find a local grower from whom to buy corn early in the morning just after it's been picked. Corn sugar begins to convert to starch as soon as the ears are harvested, but if refrigerated and cooked the same day, the corn will still be excellent to the taste.

Today, even with supersweet corns, each batch will differ in ripeness. As a general rule, corn retains its sweetness and crispness with very little cooking. Heat speeds the conversion of sugar to starch, so the more the corn is cooked, the tougher it will be. Plunge fresh, shucked corn into boiling water for a couple of minutes. For a different, yet rich texture and taste, ears of corn with their husks on can be soaked in cold water for thirty minutes, then roasted on an outdoor grill. The ears should be placed over very low or indirect heat for about twenty minutes, and turned several times.

Corn "smut" or "devil's corn," known as *cuitlacoche* in Mexico, is a grayish black fungus that grows on ears of corn, especially during a rainy summer. This fungus, *Ustilago maydis*, has been treasured for centuries. It was the Aztecs who gave it the descriptive but unflattering name of *cuitlatl* (excrement) and *cochtli* (asleep), from the Nahuatl words. It also is known to have been eaten by the Hopi as well as the Zuni, who thought it had medicinal powers. If collected when young and tender, *cuitlacoche* is considered such a delicacy that it is called "corn truffle"; it has a wonderful earthy and smoky taste. *Cuitlacoche* has been introduced only recently in restaurants outside the Southwest as a specialty in soups, crepes, puddings, salads, and other dishes. Most corn varieties are resistant to fungi, and American farmers make an effort to control corn smut, but there are always exceptions. One may find this delight growing in one's own garden or in the field of a neighboring farmer.

Cuitlacoche *Preparation*

3 tablespoons canola oil
2 tablespoons onion, finely chopped
2 garlic cloves, chopped
4 chilies poblanos; stems, veins, and seeds removed; sliced into 1/4 inch strips
6 cups cuitlacoche
kosher salt to taste

1. Remove husks and cornsilk from ears of corn and discard.
2. Cut off the fungus along with any attached corn kernels, as close to the core as possible. Chop roughly.
3. Heat oil in a frying pan. Add onion and garlic and cook until translucent.
4. Add chilies and cook for about 1 minute more.
5. Add the cuitlacoche *and salt, cover the pan, and cook over low heat for about 15 minutes, shaking the pan from time to time. The* cuitlacoche *should be tender and moist, but not soft and mushy.*

Note: If the cuitlacoche *seems dry, sprinkle a little water on it before covering. If it is too juicy, remove the lid when almost done, increase heat, and reduce the liquid.*

Yield: About 5 cups for use in recipes

An example of corn smut on some local 'Silver Queen' *that I picked in August.*

A display of new potatoes photographed in early July. You can see from the size and condition of the leaves on the complete plant that its flowers have not yet formed. The young tubers are a bit small, but full of flavor. These are 'King Edward'. To their right are 'Arran Pilot,' heirlooms that are drought-resistant and can stay in the ground with thin skins longer than most other white potatoes.

The winning combination of early summer — if you can get the ingredients to ripen at the same time. Fresh peas, new potatoes, and a little spearmint for flavor are a meal in themselves. Of course, some roast lamb also would be nice.

The "white" potato — as opposed to the sweet potato — is native to the Andes, and was developed because grains would not grow at such high altitudes. It is thought to have been a food source as early as 4000 B.C., and is known to have been widely cultivated by the time of the Incas. The first Europeans to see the potato were probably Pizarro's men. One of them, Picro de Ciezo de Leon, wrote about it in his *Chronicle of Peru*, published in 1553. It is believed he brought the potato back to Spain.

The potato did not immediately become popular in Europe, where it was regarded with suspicion and thought to be poisonous. At first it was fed to livestock. Not until the end of the 18th century did it become a staple for the poor. It also took time to be accepted in the United States. Today, of course, it is one of the world's most important foods.

Potatoes are widely grown, and you can go to your local farm stand or farmer's market to get a good selection of standards. However, there is one compelling reason to take the time and effort to grow them on your own land: the pleasure of eating tiny new potatoes fresh from the ground.

They are so tender at this stage that the skin comes away with only the slightest pressure if you rub them between your thumb and forefinger, as my daughter demonstrates.

Potatoes like well-drained spots with plenty of sunshine, but are not too demanding and will do well in most soils rich in organic matter if not too alkaline. Potatoes need nitrogen, so it is helpful to prepare the ground in the previous fall by digging in decomposed manure or compost. "Seed"potatoes may be purchased from farm stores. Catalogues, however, usually offer a wider choice of the older and heirloom varieties, specially grown and treated against disease, allowing you to experience new colors, shapes, and eating qualities.

These middle-aged, or ripe, potatoes are being gently dug up in late summer.

For purposes of garden planning, note that three pounds of seed potatoes will plant one ten-foot row, fifteen square feet, or twelve hills. The best seed potatoes are small, contain one or more eyes, and do not need cutting. If cutting is necessary, leave plenty of flesh around the eyes, since plants must live on this stored food while sprouting. Two to four weeks before the last spring frost, place tubers, or pieces of tubers, about one foot apart and eight inches deep. Cover with a few inches of earth, then apply a mulch of leaves, hay, or peat to keep the soil moist and cool and the tubers from exposure to sunlight. Potatoes that are exposed to sunlight turn green and develop a toxic substance called solanin. As the plants grow, keep mulching around the stems to form a hill and make sure they receive enough water. Fertilize plants before they flower. Good garden companions for potatoes are beans, corn, cabbage, and eggplant.

Leafy vines will rise above ground and clusters of potatoes will form below. After blossoms appear, check for the new potatoes — the size of cherries — which should be ready about sixty days after planting. Dig carefully to avoid damaging the plant and tender potatoes. If you leave them alone, they will continue to grow and the skins will harden. Our favorite way to cook tiny potatoes is to boil them gently, rolling them in a little butter and adding salt. This allows their delicate flavor to come through unmasked.

This is a traditonal formal cottage garden, established before the days of Rototillers — and easy to weed.

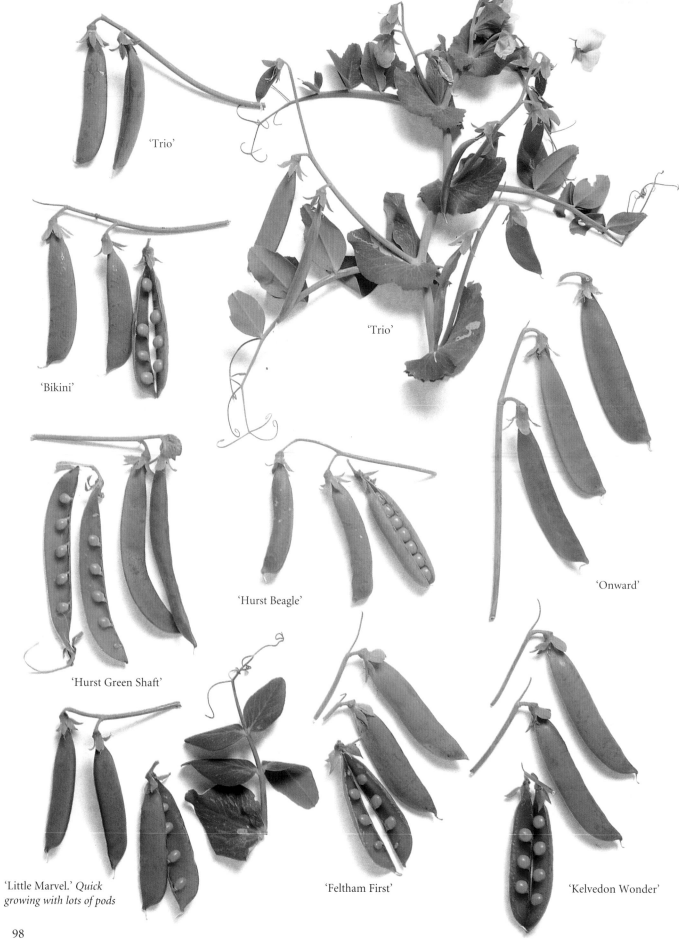

'Trio'

'Trio'

'Bikini'

'Onward'

'Hurst Beagle'

'Hurst Green Shaft'

'Little Marvel.' *Quick growing with lots of pods*

'Feltham First'

'Kelvedon Wonder'

Our second, late-season crop of 'Little Marvel.'

Peas are one of our most ancient crops, along with wheat and barley. Archaeologists have found peas in various Neolithic villages where people first domesticated plants and animals. Ripe peas were dried, commonly made into soup or porridge, and stored for use when other food was scarce. Some varieties of peas were also eaten fresh. By 1597, the famous English botanist Gerard recorded a type of *mangetout* — what we call snow peas or sugar snaps — with tender and edible pods.

My feeling is that we should take the time and effort to grow edibles, such as peas just off the vine, that we have a hard time getting any other way. The best way to experience the superb taste of fresh peas is to pick them yourself at the right moment and eat them as soon as possible; they are so sweet that you can enjoy both the small peas and the edible-pod varieties as raw snacks.

Peas grow well in cold weather. They can be planted as soon as the ground can be worked in the spring (but the soil must not be too wet or the seeds will rot). As soon as the plants are up, the roots need to be kept cool and moist with a heavy mulch, which also has the added benefit of keeping weeds down. In very warm regions it is best to grow peas during fall, winter, and early spring months. Peas like soil with a good amount of organic matter as well as a neutral pH, from 6.0 to 6.8. They also like phosphorus, which can be added by an application of bone meal, and potassium, which can be provided by wood ash.

There are dwarf varieties and tall climbing varieties; the latter will need support. I like the climbing varieties because the peas get more sun and will tend to escape the earth-loving slugs. Nothing fancy is needed — basic chicken wire fixed to stakes will do. Set up the stakes before planting in order not to disturb the new plants. Peas do well in the garden next to carrots, cucumbers, beans, and potatoes, but should not be planted next to onions or garlic.

Remember to pick peas young — the pods should be well filled but not yet hard — since a couple of extra days can turn sweet peas tough and starchy. Harvest edible-podded varieties when tender and just beginning to swell out with very tiny peas, or the pods will become chewy. If you have a generous crop, peas freeze easily and will be a treat months later.

Some recommended heirloom shelling peas are: 'Alderman' (tall telephone), 'Alaska,' 'Lincoln,' and 'Little Marvel.' Edible-podded peas include 'Dwarf Gray Sugar' and 'Mammoth Melting Sugar.' Check seed catalogues for others.

The beans grown most often in vegetable gardens today are members of the species *Phaseolus vulgaris* that originated in the Americas and were probably first cultivated thousands of years ago. Known as snap beans, common beans, kidney beans, French beans, garden beans, and filet beans, they vary in growing habits, seed and pod size, and color. Some may be dwarf, or bush, beans, while others are climbing, or pole, beans. Over the years, plantsmen have worked to produce snap beans that are "stringless" — at least when young — and therefore more pleasing to our palates. Below are some broad beans. On the right are French beans.

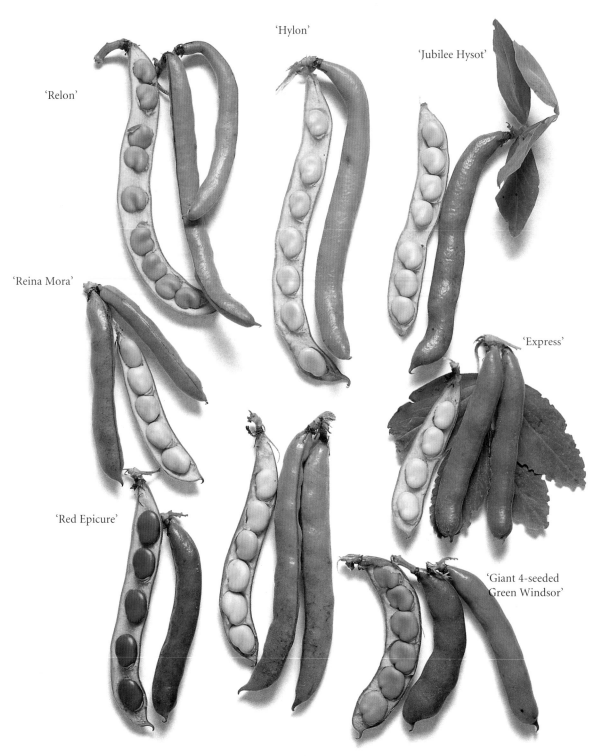

'Hylon'

'Jubilee Hysot'

'Relon'

'Reina Mora'

'Express'

'Red Epicure'

'Giant 4-seeded
Green Windsor'

'Jumbo'

'Daisy'

'Cyrus'

'Constanza'

'Delinel'

'Loch Ness'

'Tendercrop'

'Masterpeice'

'Pros Gitana'

'Royal Burgundy'

101

I suggest adding snap beans to your garden plot not only for the pleasure of eating them when they are young and tender, but also to improve your soil. Nitrogen, a valuable plant food, is added to the soil by bacteria in nodules growing on the roots of the plants. The bacteria absorb nitrogen from the air, and the nitrogen remains to enrich the earth long after the beans are harvested. And, as gardening manuals advise, by rotating the planting of beans, new areas can be enriched every year.

Try bush beans in a sunny spot in your first gardening year, since they are the easiest beans to grow and require no support. Beans will succeed in most types of soil as long as it is not too acid and has been enriched with manure or compost. Seeds must be planted in well-drained, warm soil; they will not germinate in wet, chill weather. Don't rush to plant; wait until conditions are right. Unless you want a large supply all at once to can or freeze, plant one row at a time as seedlings begin to show above ground. A constant harvest is thus provided during the entire growing season in your area. Beans do not grow well next to the onion family, but do like carrots and cucumbers as neighbors.

Keep picking the small, tender beans so that plants will continue to produce new pods. However, don't despair if harvesting is delayed and pods grow to full size; beans can be dried for winter use. Leave the plants in the ground until the bean pods are partially dried, pull them, tie them in bunches, then hang them, roots up, in a dry, well-ventilated spot. When the pods are thoroughly dry, shell the beans and store in glass canning jars.

Among the heirloom bush beans you may want to try are: 'Black Valentine,' 'Red Valentine,' 'Tendergreen,' 'Masterpiece,' 'Canadian Wonder,' 'Bountiful,' 'Royalty Purple Pod,' 'Idaho Refugee,' and 'Black Coco.'

Poles being made ready for 'Scarlet Runner,' *the most popular back-garden beans in Britain.*

These are our 'Scarlet Runner' *beans. The hummingbirds love them.*

When driving through the countryside in the summer, one often sees wild **carrot**, or Queen Anne's lace, growing along the roads and in the fields. The English colonists brought the carrot to this country, and it is believed that wild carrots are escapees from 17th-century vegetable gardens. Carrots, first cultivated in the eastern Mediterranean area, come in shapes and sizes ranging from round to short and thin to long and thick. Although we are most familiar with sweet orange carrots, others have been developed in a variety of colors including yellow, red, white, and crimson.

Soil type dictates which carrots will grow best in your area. If you have light, loose soil you can try long, slender ones, but if you have heavy or stony soil you will be more successful with shorter varieties. The soil will need to be turned over deeply with a garden fork to loosen it. Next, work in seasoned manure or compost and remove stones. At the same time, heavy clay soils can be improved with the addition of a substantial helping of sand.

Carrots are hardy and need approximately sixty-five days to mature. The first ones can be sown early, followed by additional sowings at intervals. Make the last sowing forty to sixty days before a killing frost is expected. Soak the seeds overnight to speed germination, then drain and mix the tiny seeds with sand to help space them apart evenly. It is beneficial for carrots to grow next to chives, onions, leeks, and sage, since these plants act as repellents to the carrot rust fly, whose larvae will attack young roots. When the seedlings are up, thin carefully, spacing the strongest plants three inches apart. A bumper crop can be stored in a box of slightly moist sand in a very cool place, such as a root cellar. The green tops should be cut off and the carrots should be free of soft spots or cuts, which encourage rot.

If you are interested in sampling a bit of history, you might want to plant 'Early Scarlet Horn,' a short carrot (2 to 6 inches) developed in the early 17th century and still available. Other heirlooms of interest are: 'Touchon' (6 to 8 inches), 'Danvers Half Long' (6 to 8 inches), 'Oxheart' (5 to 6 inches), 'Belgium White' (8 to 10 inches), 'Imperator' (8 to 9 inches), 'Long Orange Improved' (11 to 12 inches), and 'Rondo' (round, 1 to 2 inches).

Queen Anne's lace and carrot flower

'Berlicum Berjo'

'Cluseed New Model'

'Nandrin'

'Supreme'

'Comet'

'Autumn King Vita Longa'

'Campestra'

'Cardinal'

'Red Salad Bowl'

'Lollo Verde'

'Lollo Russo'

'Salad Bowl'

'Royal Oak Leaf'

Lettuce was known to have been cultivated by the ancient Egyptians. Early lettuce, developed from a wild species, looked very different from lettuce today since it had a tall central stalk producing leaves. In fact, our lettuce may be remembering its origins when it bolts and sends up a seed stalk. Lettuce is thought to have come to Britain with the Romans. By the 16th century, varieties of headed lettuce were recorded. Early colonists brought seeds to this country and, of course, our famous gardener, Thomas Jefferson, grew lettuce at Monticello.

It's easy to grow many wonderful varieties of lettuce in the garden, not only all those seen in the high-priced mesclun salad bins but also those rarely seen even in green markets. The principal types are the true head, or crisphead, of which the tasteless iceberg is the most familiar; butterhead, which forms a loose head; cos, or romaine, with long oval heads; and loose-leaf, or non-heading, lettuce.

Lettuce does best in cool temperatures, so choose a planting area that receives shade, or shelter it from sun behind taller, bushier plants. If you live in an area with intense midsummer heat and a long growing season, plant in early spring and again in late summer. When you order seeds, read the descriptions carefully in order to pick the varieties best suited to your conditions. In general, loose-leaf lettuce is the most resistant to bolting

Here is properly spaced lettuce that I grew from seedlings.

'Merveille des Quatre Saisons'

'Waldeman's Green'

'Green Ice'

'Goya'

'Carioka'

'Alda'

from heat and takes the shortest time to mature — around forty days. Also, sow new rows every couple of weeks to provide a constant supply. A good shortcut for growing headed lettuce is to buy seedlings from your local nursery. Make certain that they've been "hardened off" — left outside for a few days to acclimate — before planting. Transplant in the late afternoon when the sun is low, then water well. These precautions will make certain that your plants experience the least amount of stress.

For the best lettuce, soil should be properly drained, rich in organic material, and not too acidic. Our garden is in an area with no natural limestone, so we need to "sweeten" the earth every season with lime in order to grow most things well. Soil can be tested with a home pH test. Moisture is essential to growing lettuce, so water regularly in dry spells. Harvest loose-leaf lettuce by picking the larger outside leaves, leaving the young center to grow new leaves. To harvest headed lettuce the entire plant must be pulled up.

Here are some of the heirloom varieties available today: Leaf: 'Black Seeded Simpson,' 'Red Oak Leaf,' 'Red Deer Tongue,' 'Bronze Arrow.' Romaine: 'Paris White Cos,' 'Rouge d'Hiver,' 'Balloon.' Butterhead: 'May King,' 'Tom Thumb,' 'Merveille des Quatre Saisons,' 'Grandpa Admires,' 'Brune d'Hiver,' 'Limestone Bibb,' 'Tennis Ball.' Head: 'Hanson,' 'Continuity Red Crisphead,' 'Reine des Glaces.'

Fall lettuce grown from seed sown in mid-August.

Squash and **pumpkins**, with their trailing or climbing vines, are all members of the large genus *Cucurbita*, and as with many other plants described here, are native to the Americas. Plant historians believe that they were first cultivated for their seeds and later for their flesh. Gardeners usually think of them either as summer squash, to be eaten while their skins are tender, or winter squash and pumpkins, which remain on the vine until the rinds are hard.

The seeds you select will come from four main species. All the jokes about size and quantity, along with dozens of special cookbooks, refer to *Cucurbita Pepo*. This species includes zucchini, crookneck, pattypan, and acorn squash, and some pumpkins. *C. maxima* covers the winter squashes: 'Buttercup,' Hubbard, turban, and 'Banana,' plus the true, or "French," pumpkins. *C. moschata* includes the popular 'Butternut,' one of the winter crooknecks. *C. mixta*, grown mostly in the Southwest because of its drought tolerance, includes the 'Green-Striped Cushaw.'

'Zenith'

'Early Butternut'

'Ponca'

Gooseneck

'Sweet Dumpling'

'Delicata'

'Waltham But

'Clarita'

'Supremo'

'All Green Bush'

'Table Dainty'

'Burpee Golden'

'Minipak'

'Tiger Cross'

'Tender and True'

107

One eight-seed hill begins to expand from the garden and follows the sun onto the lawn.

Pumpkins and squash are known as "heavy feeders," so dig in plenty of compost and dried manure. Don't give in to the temptation to sow seeds too early, because they will not germinate well — or at all — in cold soil. (I must confess I've done this in my enthusiasm to get everything going in the spring.) It's better to start some seeds indoors and transplant when the soil temperature has warmed. As a beginning gardener I planted in rows, but now I make hills about ten inches high and three feet apart. Each hill gets six to eight seeds. Later I thin to the two strongest seedlings. Mulch under the vines to retain moisture, protect the fruit, and keep the weeds down.

At an earlier stage, the same planting as at top shows its potential.

Summer squash have the best taste and texture when small, but if there are some clunkers, don't feel guilty about not eating them. Just toss them on the compost heap. Take winter squash and pumpkins off the vine before frost, then cure them in the sun or in a warm, well-ventilated place for a week. If curing outside, you will need to cover them at night to protect against frost. Store in a dry place at around 55°F. And remember to add the vines to your compost heap.

There are many heirloom varieties of squash and pumpkins available. Here are a few you might want to try: Summer: 'Yellow Crookneck,' 'Cocozelle Zucchini,' 'Black Zucchini,' 'White Bush Scallop.' Winter: 'Blue Hubbard,' 'Delicata,' 'Hopi Orange,' 'Blue Banana,' 'Boston Marrow,' 'Butternut,' 'Acorn Table Queen.' Pumpkins for decoration: 'Rouge Vif d'Etampess,' 'Connecticut.' Field Pumpkins for pies: 'Small Sugar,' 'Winter Luxury,' 'Seminole,' 'White Rind Sugar.'

A friend of mine who is an expert gardener cut off a squash stalk, blew into it and made it sound like a tenor saxophone.

In Delaware, pattypan squash was sliced through like this, then dipped in flour along with little soft-shell crabs of the same size and thickness. They were then fried together in butter, making the crabs 'go further.'

When the Shakers invented the seed packet, they introduced the notion of sowing thinly. They put into each packet just enough seeds for a family plot. The instructions on the back of the packet and the handbook they produced supplied simple information without idealized imagery. Today commercial seedsmen present glossy pictures with even bigger and shinier specimens than the ones we collected and cleaned up for these pages. The truth about tastier vegetables is being told by the heirloom seed enthusiasts and the independent suppliers, in catalogues that look as though they were designed and illustrated by talented local friends who support the cause. Most importantly, these catalogues are a good read, full of opinions, anecdotes, and recipes — all of which inspire trust.

Some good-quality independent and family-owned publications

The 1997 Ethnobotanical Catalog of Seeds

CATALOG No. 58
JANUARY 1997
PRICE: $1.00

'Vectors'
Concept & design by J.L. Hudson.
Drawing executed by Davis Te Selle.

J. L. HUDSON, SEEDSMAN
Star Route 2, Box 337
La Honda, California, 94020 USA

Send Catalog Requests ONLY to: P. O. Box 1058, Redwood City, CA 94064 USA

Established 1911 by H. E. Saier.
"Don't buy what you don't need."—H. E. Saier, 1973.

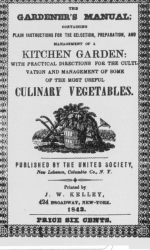

Cabbage: Cures to Cuisine

Judith Hiatt

...rs ago I read an amazing book by a French herbalist. It was he who ...ned my mind to the marvels of the humble cabbage. It was one of ...favorite remedies and he used its gentle leaves with expertise - making ...wonder how he knew about cabbage's magic. It's all here in this ...k! How to grow it - a review of all the different types of cabbages in ...garden. The recipes even include one of my family's heritage which ...called "Berrocks" and called krautburger in this book. There is a recipe ...sauerkraut chocolate cake which I have tasted and is delicious (no ...ding!) as well as many more conventional that equally tasty recipes. ...remedies section is invaluable. Did you know that cabbage or its ...e will offset the effects of too much wine? This is an amazing ...ection of information about cabbage.
...tcover..122 pages.................................$8.50

Brassica oleracea var. acephala

This is a "gardener's only" crop! You won't get the point if you buy collards from the supermarket. Only after gathering them from a nippy spring or fall garden will you know why these greens have become country favorites. Cook them quickly (steam or stirfry) over high heat. Garlic, onions, and parboiled potatoes are nice but unnecessary additions.

Soil Temp: 45-95F.....(North: plant June 15 for fall harv)......Harv in 8-9 wks
Spacing: Plants-24".......................Rows-36"...........................Intensive-24"
Packets contain about 440 seeds and plant approximately 32'
VATES......................Cook top clusters...R
MORRIS IMPROVED HEADING............Excellent flavor...................R
SOUTHERN.............Good in hot or cold weather.........................R

*=Heirloom; R/P=Regular/Preservation pkt [see pg 2, #8]; Packets $2.65

Arugula/Rocket
Eruca vesicaria

A quick flash in the garden, rocket should be planted once a week so the leaves may be continually gathered at the tenderest young stage (under 2-3"). It adds a nutty dimension with a peppery bite to salads. It is best grown in spring and fall. Once the plants flower, the leaves turn bitter. Grown well and gathered at the right moment, they add a fullness to salads that will alter history both in your kitchen and for the gardener (no effort will be spared to get these tender leaves to the chef!).

Plant very early spring and again in the fall................Harvest in 6 weeks
Spacing: Plants-6"......................Rows-18".......................Intensive-6"
Packets contain about 520 seeds and plant approximately 10'
*ARUGULA/ITALIAN CRESS.............Young leaves for salads...........R

Black and white **pepper**corns, or *Piper nigrum*, were so prized for seasoning and medicinal use that, as far back as ancient Greek and Roman times and up through the Middle Ages, they were used as currency. So it is not surprising that when explorers of the New World brought back the species *Capsicum annuum*, which includes the sweet peppers and the hot pepper, it was quickly accepted and grown. Hot peppers were dried and used in place of the costly spices from the East Indies.

Sweet peppers, also called pimentos, have been a popular vegetable in kitchen gardens for years. Catalogues offer a wide variety of shapes and sizes, with tastes ranging from the very sweet — good for eating raw — to those better for frying, roasting, or stuffing. Only recently, however, have many of us also become familiar with the hot peppers used in cooking the foods of India, Thailand, Mexico, and China. We lovers of chili peppers can grow many kinds in our own gardens. Their heat depends both on the variety of pepper and on the weather — the hotter the weather, the hotter the pepper.

If your growing season is short, select early varieties — even these take about two months to mature after young plants are set out. Unless you have the right indoor conditions and are around to give regular attention, it is probably wiser to buy seedlings than to start them yourself. A local nursery may even be willing to grow from seed the special varieties you want to try. Once the soil is warm, and either in the evening or on a cloudy day, plant in a normally sunny spot, and water well. Most garden guides recommend placing a paper cup with its bottom removed around each stem to protect the young plant from cutworms. Mulch around the plants to keep the soil moist and to aid fruit formation.

Harvest peppers at any stage, but the longer they are left on the plant, the sweeter or hotter they will become. For winter cooking, we have frozen bumper crops of sweet peppers and jalapeños with great success. Here's how: Wash and dry thoroughly, then core and remove seeds and white membrane. Cut into quarters, place in plastic bags and store in the freezer. Or dice the peppers, flash-freeze on a tray for a few minutes, then pack into containers or bags for freezer storage. Mature hot peppers also can be dried: thread them on a string through the stems and hang outdoors in the dry Southwest, or elsewhere indoors in a sunny window. When dry, the pods are dark and will bend without snapping.

Here are a few of the heirloom varieties currently advertised in catalogues: Sweet: 'Nardello,' 'Figaro Sweet Italian,' 'Red & Yellow Cornos,' 'Bull Nose,' 'Cherry Sweet,' 'Golden Summit,' 'Sweet Banana,' 'World Beater,' 'Merrimack Wonder.' Hot: 'Aci Sivri,' 'Large Red Cherry Hot,' 'Ancho' (Poblano), 'Tabasco,' 'Tepin,' 'Serrano,' 'Habanero' (Scotch Bonnet), 'Thai Hot Pasilla,' 'Mulato,' 'Chili de Arbol,' 'Bulgarian Carrot,' 'Chimayo,' 'Czechoslovakian Black,' 'De Comida,' 'Long Red Cayenne,' 'Pico de Gallo.'

'Clio'

'Purple Belle'

'Gypsy'

'Hot Gold Spike'

'Cayenne'

'Serrano'

'Red Chili'

111

Sweet potatoes

had been in a slow decline until recent years, when innovative young chefs turned their attention to American food. Many people thought of them as coming from a can, covered with sugar and marshmallows, and appearing on the Thanksgiving dinner table. They had never tasted traditional baked sweet potatoes mashed with butter and pepper, or hot sweet potato biscuits, spicy pie, or chips. Now sweet potatoes are making a comeback, and they're easy to grow if you have the right conditions.

Sweet potatoes (*Ipomoea Batatas*) — no relation to the true potato — are also native to South and Central America. They are not yams, which, if you get them at all, are expensive imports from Africa. As you might guess, they like hot weather and a long growing season, but it is possible to grow them in the North if you plant them in a sun-drenched area and cover the soil with black plastic for extra warmth. We have had successful crops at the end of a hot summer here in Zone 5 — and unsuccessful crops, too. One year our sweet potatoes, although healthy, were long and thin instead of plump. My research revealed that this result was caused by too much rain late in the season.

Buy sweet potato "slips," or rooted sprouts, from your local nursery or from a mail-order catalogue; plant after all danger of frost has passed and the soil has warmed. Push the soil along your row into ridges ten inches high (one long hill) and set the slips about one foot apart. The rows need to be three feet apart to allow room for the vines to spread. Sweet potatoes don't require a lot of extra care, but they do need regular watering until they are established.

In the North, dig sweet potatoes immediately when there are frost warnings; otherwise the plants will wilt and turn black. In warmer areas, harvest after about 120 days. Dig the tubers carefully to avoid damaging the skins, and then lay them out on newspapers to dry in a warm spot for a couple of weeks. They should be stored in a cool, dry place (55°F), layered between straw or peat moss, to be enjoyed all winter.

Sweet potatoes are either moist-fleshed with a deep orange color or dry-fleshed with a pale orange color. Some have now been developed for northern areas, with a 90- to 100-day maturity — earlier than the traditional 120-day growing period.

Sweet potato cultivars

Another tuber that originated in Peru is the 'Cassava,' also known as 'Tapioca,' 'Manioc,' or 'Manihot.' Although I remember it from the dreadful tapioca pudding, it is a very fine source of starch. In the U.S. it is also grown as food for livestock.

In our northern climate, # Brussels sprouts
and kale are the last two green vegetables to soldier on in the garden — hardy through frost and even snow — and we have been able to serve ours at Thanksgiving. In warmer areas, brussels sprouts are usually planted in late summer so that they can be picked from December through February. As you might guess, this vegetable was first developed in Belgium, reaching England and America in the early 1800s. The heirloom varieties are generally thought to have a much better flavor than more recently developed ones; Bedford Fillbasket is one of the traditionals you might want to try.

'Rubine'

'Bedford Fillbasket'

'Early Half Tall'

The raised beds of 17th-century gardening at Plimoth Plantation.

Some 18th-century formal vegetable plots at rest in Lancaster County, Pennsylvania.

Beans coming up in a re-created slave garden in Virginia.

Herb cutting at Plimoth.

'Albion'

'Staro'

'Kurenai Red'

'Rosso di Firenze'

'The Kelsae'

Onions always let you know when they are ready. I photographed these in mid-September. They were gathered and strung just before the first frost.

Onions and garlic belong to the

genus *Allium.* If you were blindfolded, you could probably identify them by odor alone. Both have been used throughout history as medicinal remedies for everything from colds and indigestion to earaches and insect stings. Common "globe" onions have papery outer skins of various colors — white, red, brown, and red or purple — depending on the type. Onions and garlic are rewarding to harvest and keep but require a long growing season, so most gardeners plant "sets," or small bulbs, to shorten the time to maturity — about three to four months. Just don't put them next to peas or beans, whose growth they inhibit.

The look of home-grown garlic.

117

Cucumbers

Cucumbers are reported to have been cultivated in India three thousand years ago, with their wild origin in the northern mountains of that country. They now come in many shapes and sizes, ranging from tiny French cornichons to those as long as eighteen inches. To grow well, cucumbers require a rich soil, warm weather, and plenty of water. And, once the plants are fruiting, all edible cucumbers must be picked so that flowering and fruiting will continue. Unless you want lots of pickles, two or three plants are more than enough for one family.

'Bush Champion'

'Telegraph Improved'

'Burpless Tasty Green'

'Kyoto'

The purple pear-shaped eggplant was the kind commonly seen in markets and in seed catalogues until cuisines from China, India, and Thailand became so popular in this country. Now we see many varieties, ranging from white egg-shaped and small orange to long, slender green fruits. The eggplant is believed to be a native of eastern Asia, where it was cultivated at least four thousand years ago, and to have been introduced to Europe by the Moors in Andalusia. As with several other vegetables mentioned here, the eggplant was slow to gain acceptance in Europe and the United States. The first varieties were grown more as ornamentals than as vegetables.

Eggplants, like peppers and tomatoes, belong to the nightshade family and need the same hot weather, rich soil, and long growing season — 100 to 120 days from seed. In colder areas it will be helpful to set out seedlings only after the soil is warm, and then to mulch with black plastic to hold the sun's heat in the soil.

Heirloom varieties currently available through catalogues include: 'Black Beauty,' 'Pingtung Long,' 'Rosa Bianca,' 'Thai Green,' 'Turkish Orange,' and 'Violetta di Firenze.'

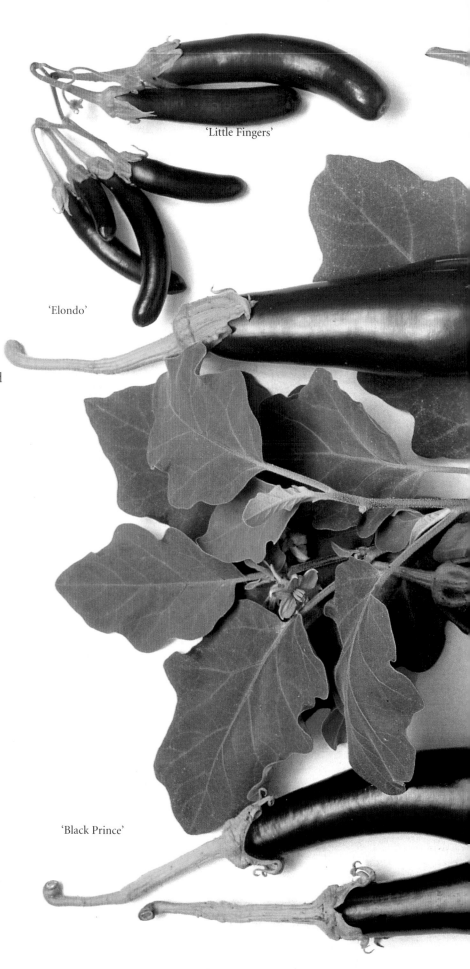

'Little Fingers'

'Elondo'

'Black Prince'

'Rima'

'Slice Rite'

'Black Enorma'

Keeping the garden harvest

Root Cellars

When you grow your own vegetables it's a shame to think they must always be eaten immediately, given away, frozen, or — most ridiculous of all (and I've done it) — thrown on the compost heap. Reviving or making a root cellar to store produce out of season is a worthwhile project. Your own produce always tastes better than the supermarket versions of the same.

If you have the right conditions — a temperature between 33°F and 45°F and humidity between sixty and seventy percent — you can keep fruit and vegetables in boxes, barrels, or even heaps if they are buried in dry sand or straw. The secret is to keep everything separated. We all know how one bruised apple will affect another; before very long, rot sets in. And a root cellar can store more than just roots.

Onions, garlic, and shallots

Pull these up after the tops have fallen over, brush off excess dirt, and place in the sun for a few days to harden and dry. Then cut off the tops and place produce in mesh bags for ventilation. (Nylon mesh laundry bags are excellent and can be washed and reused.) Store in a very cool, dry area. Or, for a decorative solution, leave the tops on, braid them, and hang them in the cellar, keeping a few strands at a time in the kitchen, ready for use.

Apples and pears

These two fruits keep very well in a root cellar but need to be separated from other vegetables because they tend to absorb odors. Pick when mature but still hard and only put away perfect apples or pears, those without nicks, soft spots, or other blemishes. Let them cool overnight to lose the heat of the sun, then wrap individually in newspaper.

Place them in corrugated or wooden boxes or barrels, make a bed of hay or straw, and add hay or straw between each layer of fruit. Top off with more hay or straw. The ideal storage temperature is right at 32°F, so if you don't have a root cellar, check the temperature in an unheated basement or ordinary cellar.

Beets, carrots, potatoes, turnips
There are several effective methods for storing these root vegetables, which should be harvested in the fall when the soil is relatively dry. Brush off the dirt but do not wash. For carrots, beets, and turnips, leave the root end and about 1/2 inch at the top when cutting off the leaves. Pack between layers of lightly moist sand or peat in crates and baskets, or in corrugated cartons that have been lined with plastic bags with plenty of small air holes. Carrots and turnips (as well as leeks) also can be left in the ground and covered with a foot-deep layer of hay or

straw after the ground freezes. They can be dug as needed throughout the winter. As for potatoes, dig carefully to avoid cuts and nicks, and then leave on the ground to air-dry for several hours. Put in crates or boxes and cover lightly to keep out all light. The vegetables then can be stored in a humid but well-ventilated root cellar or unheated basement maintained at a temperature between 35°F and 40°F. Leave a pail of water in the area to provide extra humidity, if necessary.

Pumpkins, Hubbard and butternut squash
Cut fruits off the vine before frost, leaving a couple of inches of stem. Let them dry in the sun for about two weeks to harden the rind, but cover at night if frost is predicted. Store in a basement, attic, or root cellar where the temperature is between 50°F and 60°F. It is best to keep individual fruits separate, in rows, rather than in a big heap.

In the South, the harvest was sometimes dried. Hanging on the kitchen wall are carefully sliced beans, tomatoes, peppers, apples, squash, and pumpkins.

I know from personal experience that it is hard to stop birds from attacking raspberries. My friend has built a wire-roofed-and-walled cage for his canes.

There's a moment in high summer when, along with the garden vegetables, all the fruit seems to ripen at the same time. Then the wasps arrive to circle over the unpicked berries. Unfortunately, there is a limit to what one can pick and eat on the same day. The answer is to freeze — which works well for raspberries and blueberries — or make jam.

Strawberries

We love strawberries but have never felt the need to grow them ourselves. Wonderful tiny wild ones — *fraises de bois* — with an intense flavor grow all across our big field. Also there are local farmers who cultivate strawberries as a specialty crop — picking them as they ripen. At their stands you can buy quarts; or for big projects like jam and freezing, you can pick berries right from the field at a very reasonable price, especially if you bring your own basket.

Raspberries

Somewhere on your property, it is quite likely that you will find a neglected patch of red raspberries that can be brought back to full production with pruning and care.

If not, think about planting canes and establishing a patch. Plants need minimum care: a well-drained sunny spot, slightly acidic soil, a bit of fertilizer, pruning, and a few nets to protect ripe fruit from the birds. We found raspberries on a sunny slope in the field nearest our house and their scent fills the air on hot summer days. In a good year, when the weather cooperates, there are so many raspberries that we not only have them for breakfast and dinner, but also make jam, raspberry vinegar, and raspberry liqueur. Then we quickly freeze extras in single layers on baking sheets and place them in bags to store for winter pies, muffins, and pancakes.

Rhubarb

Rhubarb, often called "pie plant" in old texts because of its popularity as a pie filling, is a hardy vegetable perennial that can live for many years. We keep it outside the garden where it has plenty of room to grow undisturbed. After winter dormancy, the tall red or green stalks topped with large leaves come up in the spring and continue growing into the summer.

I never liked rhubarb when I was young. It seemed to turn up every week at school lunches — mushy, sour, and overcooked. Now I prefer to think of it as deliciously astringent in desserts, sorbets, jams, and chutneys. Rhubarb stalks freeze well with no loss of flavor, so large amounts can be harvested and stored until you choose to deal with them.

'Early Victoria'

'Timperley Early'

'Stockbridge Cropper'

'The Sutton'

'Cawood Castle'

'Hawkes' Champagne'

'Early Cherry'

Blueberries

Blueberries are also very rewarding to grow. They do not need a great deal of attention but to do really well must have a very acidic soil with sufficient sun and moisture. Along the path to our pond, we planted bushes of six varieties for good pollination and continuous ripening throughout the summer. In our northern growing zone, the early blueberries are usually ripe by midsummer and the latest ones by September. You will find that berries maturing on the bushes really are superior in taste. In the autumn, the leaves turn reddish and present a strong contrast to the brown field.

Apples

Nearly everyone inherits at least a couple of overgrown trees that still produce small apples. Sometimes the trees can be pruned back slowly, over several years, for better fruit; but if not, the apples are usually still good for making chutney, jam, applesauce, or cider. And, in any case, the trees give a colorful display of blossoms in the spring. Our ambitious plans to restore an entire orchard were scaled back to the reality of caring for a few trees, and we still have more than enough apples for one family. Old orchards still attract many deer to our area.

Yellow and red plums are ready to be turned into the jam below.

A large handful of rosemary, purple and green basil, sage, Italian parsley, and thyme. They were chopped and added (with a little cream) to our chanterelles.

Sacred Basil

Herbs

Purple Basil

'Green Ruffles'

Basil

This annual with bright green leaves is probably today's most popular herb. We associate hot summer days with its fragrance, and many summer recipes call for fresh basil. Fortunately, basil grows quickly from seed and does well as long as it has plenty of sun. Seeds can be sown directly in the garden as soon as the soil is warm, and a midsummer sowing will give you small plants that can be potted and brought indoors for winter use. Basil succumbs to the first frost, so it's a good idea to make pesto for the freezer and to dry leaves in the microwave early in the summer.

Sweet Basil

Lemon Basil

Anise Scented Basil

Chervil

Pale green, lacy leaves top the small annual chervil. One of the French traditional *fines herbes* (tarragon, parsley, chives), it has a delicate taste a bit reminiscent of tarragon and is best when used fresh. Chervil can be started from seed and successive sowings will provide a continuous supply. The leaves may be frozen in small packets.

Chives

The most delicate member of the onion family is also a hardy perennial. In June, the long thin leaves are topped with edible purple-pink flowers that add a strong, peppery flavor to salads. The chives should be cut back at this time for a second crop. We have a long border in the vegetable garden providing chives to freeze, cut flowers for the house, and good compost material. Chives also grow well in pots that you can keep close to the kitchen door.

Coriander

The coriander plant is an aromatic annual whose fresh leaves and later seeds are used extensively in Indian, Chinese, and Mexican cooking. The seed, which has been used since ancient times, is an important ingredient in curry powders and spice mixtures, and also flavors breads, cakes, puddings, and other desserts. We sow several times directly into the garden for a good crop of leaves because the plant tends to bolt quickly. Leaves can be frozen on a tray and then stored in bags in the freezer.

Dill

This annual with feathery, blue-green leaves can grow as tall as three to four feet, and also will produce seeds. To have plenty of dill leaves for summer recipes and pickling, successive sowings in a sunny spot are recommended. The leaves can be dried in the microwave. Seeds should be allowed to ripen on the plant and then brought indoors for final drying.

Lovage

Although not so well-known in America, lovage is a wonderfully tall perennial — growing six to eight feet — that was popular in early Greek and Roman times and was always included in medieval monastery gardens. The young, dark green leaves with a celery-like flavor can be used in soups, stews, pastas, and salads. The leaves can be either dried or frozen.

Mint

There are many varieties of this extremely fragrant perennial. The mint outside our back door is spearmint (*Mentha spicata*), the one most commonly used for cooking. Mint grows so easily that it often becomes invasive, but we have not had that problem here in the North and especially love having mint to cook with new peas and potatoes. It needs plenty of moisture and quickly depletes the soil, so it is good to dress it with compost and bone meal. Mint freezes and dries well.

The herb garden at Ballymaloe House, County Cork, Ireland, famous for its home-grown and home-cooked fare.

Parsley

Italian parsley, with its large, flat, segmented leaves, is preferred to curly varieties for culinary purposes. The leaves freeze well in plastic containers or bags to be used as needed. The seeds take a very long time to germinate, so we always get a head start by buying plants at the nursery. Plants may be potted and brought inside for the winter, but keep them away from heat and give them some sunlight every day.

Rosemary

This pungent perennial shrub with glossy green leaves can live for years with the proper attention; it must be brought inside for the winter in cold climates. Rosemary thrives in full sun and is excellent with roasts, soups, stews, and vegetables; the plant is easily propagated from cuttings.

Common Sage

This aromatic bush with smoky gray-green leaves on woody stems becomes more and more handsome with age. It seems to have an affinity for chicken, duck, and pork, and is the traditional stuffing herb. Easy to grow, sage likes ordinary, dryish soil and plenty of sun. Its stems should be cut back every spring and the leaves harvested for drying in early summer before flower spikes appear.

Rocket, or Arugula

Arugula, or rocket, is an annual, native to the Mediterranean and eastern Asia. The strong and peppery leaves are best picked young for use raw in salads and pastas. Arugula also makes a great pesto on its own or combined with parsley or basil — and it freezes well. Arugula tends to bolt in hot weather, so that periodic sowing throughout the growing season is recommended for a plentiful supply.

Savory, Summer

Aromatic with a slightly peppery taste, this annual is often called the bean herb because of the character it lends to dishes whose base is peas, beans, or lentils. It germinates quickly when sown directly into the garden, and likes rich, light soil and plenty of sun. It dries well for winter use.

Sorrel, French

This perennial shoots up bright green leaves in our garden in the early spring. They are shield-shaped, with a lovely lemony flavor that adds tang to soups as well as sauces for meats, fish, and salads. Keep cutting back the leaves and the plants will send up new shoots all summer, as long as it is not too dry. If there is a plentiful crop, we remove the stems, cook the leaves for a few minutes in butter, then puree and freeze for sauces later.

Flat Parsley

Coriander

Curled Parsley

Tarragon, French

Different from other herbs because it does not set viable seed, French tarragon must be obtained as a plant. Further plants can be grown from cutting or by root division. It needs good drainage, likes full sun and good soil, but is hardy and can stand low winter temperatures. Tarragon is the important ingredient in tarragon vinegar, Bearnaise sauce, and many chicken, meat, and fish dishes. It keeps its strength when dried.

Thyme

There is almost no stew, soup, or ragout that does not call for a quantity of thyme. This low, spreading perennial has an ancient history as a medicinal and culinary herb, and bees are also very fond of its flowers. It is best to cut thyme for drying just before the buds appear, as the flavor is stronger then.

The Saffron Crocus

The saffron crocus grows from underground corms. Narrow leaves appear in summer, then lovely flowers in September with stigmas that hang out between the petals like orange tongues. These frail threads are dried to make colorful dyes and the well-known perfumed spice. Saffron is expensive because it takes many thousands of flowers to provide just one pound. It is possible to grow a number of plants and dry small amounts for yourself, but do a bit of research and buy the correct species.

Rocket, or Arugula

French sorrel

Wild sorrel

Large-leaved sorrel

Trees

It is sometimes difficult to understand the connection between the destruction of the rain forest, enlarging deserts, and me, when I see the steady advance of reforestation where I live. Not so long ago the deeply wooded area around me, covering hundreds of square miles, looked like the moorland described in the novel *Wuthering Heights*. Most of the land where we live had been cleared by settlers who raised sheep for the wool used in the mills of the Northeast; the rest of the forested area was turned into charcoal to fire up industrial furnaces. Our area renewed itself once people moved on, but we know this is not happening elsewhere today. Increases in population and the production of carbon dioxide are overtaking the ability of vegetation to provide balance. We need thirty percent of tree cover at all times to keep this planet healthy. So keep your trees, or use them to make more, and do us all a favor. On our own little piece of land we have, for the most part, a policy of noninterference towards the trees — 70 percent of our land is covered with them. But we keep them out of existing fields and clearings where we can. Even so, my wife has planted black walnut saplings, an endangered species, in favored spots.

We have thousands of hardwoods and conifers on our land pushing and shoving for space, though we know the big hardwoods will eventually take over and adjust themselves for the new millennium. City trees in parks, along avenues, or planted to beautify buildings, need attention — watering, pruning, and bark protection. Trees in the wild find their positions by a process of selection and can take care of themselves. But whether in the city, in the country, or in-between, people plant trees because they like them. Trees symbolize steady growth and a peaceful world and are important in our lives. In any case, one should manage the trees in the manner of the old days when folk could see the depletion around them and used trees very carefully.

A slow-growing beech tree establishes itself in a wild section of our woods.

On higher ground with more softwoods, it's easier for me to maintain mossy paths like this.

Some neatly pollarded willows in Williamstown, Massachusetts.

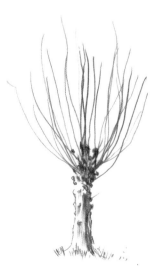

Pollarding is a way to produce smooth, straight young wood for fences, poles, and basketry, as well as for perfect stove wood. Young trees are lopped to a height of about six feet to encourage the growth of shoots. When these shoots grow to the required size and are harvested, the tree will send out more, and so on. Such operations do no harm to the plant itself, but do change its appearance. The shape of pollarded trees is familiar to lovers of landscape painting and travelers throughout Europe. Corot, the 19th-century French painter, couldn't bear to paint a tree unless it was pollarded.

In coppiced areas, wildflowers always appear around the stumps before the brush starts to move in.

Material for new fencing ready to come out of coppiced woodland.

Coppicing is similar to pollarding. In this case, a tree is cut down to a stump that sends up shoots and begins to resemble a bush. Again, after harvesting every five to ten years, there will be shoots as before. This process can continue for many years. The word "coppice" (from which we get the word "copse") originates from the French *couper*, to cut. Pollarding and coppicing are good and easy ways to manage your timber, thin out among your favorite trees, and probably keep the wildlife increasing in many areas. However, coppicing means you will have to fence off the area because deer will always graze the young shoots.

Once-pollarded crack willows in the style loved by landscape painters. They have since been properly trimmed.

A fine example of pollarded poplars trained into a windbreak.

Another, smaller windbreak for an orchard. The ashes from the pruned hardwood can go straight into the ground.

My chain saw cooling down. Cold, clear days, when the ground is hard, are the best times to use this tool.

A pair of forester's tools

*Left. Grafting froe.
The sharp point
at the top right was used
to prise open the root stock
that was to recieve the graft.
The curved indentation on
the left side of the blade is to
split the root further just
before the graft is pushed in.*

*Below. Race knife,
or timber scribe.
This was used to make
a circular incision
to mark or tap timber.*

As winter approaches and I sit by the fire, I familiarize myself with my chain saw owner's manual. I am very pleased with this powerful and necessary tool, but 3,000 feet a minute in my hands is a big responsibility.

We have many trees on our land. Inevitably some are blown down, sometimes blocking our driveway and paths. Whenever this happens, out I go, chain saw in hand.

I'm especially careful, being left-handed. The good old farm tools had an ambidextrous quality, but the modern chain saw has a right-handed view of the world, and I do not want to be one of the over 69,000 Americans every year who visit hospital emergency rooms with chain saw injuries. Car manuals may devote most of their pages to the stereo system, but my chain saw manual devotes two-thirds of its pages to safety measures.

In addition to what is in the manual, I take a few extra precautions: First, I do not wear boots with laces; second, I always have a clear exit in the event of an emergency; and finally, I never cut down a tree thicker than the length of my saw.

139

Thinning gives a grovelike quality to this birch wood in western Massachusetts.

Tree farming is a way that country dwellers with ten acres of woodland or more can become active stewards of their property by joining the American Tree Farm System. There are currently more than 73,000 tree farmers who dedicate an area of their privately owned land to this system, growing and harvesting forest crops while at the same time protecting wildlife and other natural resources.

Tree farming, or managing our forests for renewal, is a relatively new development, since man has traditionally taken what he needed and left renewal to nature. However, much of our hope for essential supplies of forest products in the years ahead lies in programs such as this, which was begun in Washington state in 1941, and became national by the following year. Since most beginning tree farmers need help, each state organization provides advice from foresters, Master Woodland Managers, and other experts.

To become certified, a prospective tree farm is inspected by a volunteer forester who donates time to the program. One must own a minimum of ten acres, even for a Christmas tree farm, and develop a written management plan. The plan can be brief and simple but it must address the landowner's goals, which should include the production of renewable crops of forest products and the protection of soil, water, aesthetics, recreation, and fish and wildlife resources. The plan is signed by the landowner, indicating that it has been requested and fits the goals intended. The forester also signs off on the plan, confirming that it is technically and environmentally sound. Foresters check the property every five years to verify adherence to the plan. Tree farmers use various forestry methods to achieve their goals:

Clear-cutting involves cutting all the trees in a specific area, and is used for types of forests that reproduce best in large spaces where seedlings will not survive in the shade of larger trees. Some forests, for example, renew

themselves naturally in clearings created by fires or wind-storms. Situations where clear-cuts are chosen are those in which insects have devastated large areas or the trees are of such condition or age that they need to be replaced by younger, healthier trees.

The *single tree* method is similar to clear-cutting except that small numbers of trees are left singly, in narrow strips or in groups, to provide seed sources for regeneration but not enough shade to kill the new seedlings.

The *shelterwood* method is used when most of the trees are the same age, as the forest nears maturity. First some trees are cut and removed to encourage growth of the remaining trees and seed production. This also lets sunlight reach the forest floor to increase the decay of organic matter. After a few years more trees are cut, letting additional sunlight reach the soil, which is the germination bed for falling seed. Thus new growth is established in the shade of the mature forest. Later cuts are made to harvest

the remaining mature trees and release the young trees into full sunlight. This method is used with species that do well in partial shade in early stages but need full sunlight as they grow. With the final removal, the forest is once again composed of trees of similar age.

When forests have trees of many different ages, other methods are used:
Group selection removes some older trees in small groups or strips, leaving enough open space to allow new trees to grow freely.

Single tree selection periodically harvests large trees, making small openings in which seedlings can establish themselves.

Improvement cutting thins out the forest and maintains good growth of quality timber by removing trees of poor quality. Trees grown by these methods have to be tolerant of partial shade, and the forest must be entered for cutting periodically.

American trees

Red Alder

The red alder is a hardwood that grows in the Pacific Northwest and is used for furniture, cabinetwork, and pulpwood. A "pioneer" tree that grows on disturbed sites, it is likely to be seen on roadsides and in moist areas. It is not good for firewood.

Ash

There are many varieties of ash. The most valuable are the American, or white, ash, the black ash and the Oregon ash, the only one native to the Northwest. White ash is valued for its strength, which makes it suitable for tool handles, sports equipment, and furniture. It also has the quality of keeping its strength even though bent, which made it perfect for wagon wheels and shafts. Ash splints well, and historically the black ash has been used for baskets, chairs, and boxes. It is interesting to note that a dye from the inner bark of the blue ash was used by early settlers to color their cloth. Oregon ash is used for furniture, flooring, and other millwork. These hardwoods provide good firewood.

Quaking Aspen

This tree is seen all across North America and grows quickly in old fields. Its wood is used mostly for pulpwood, boxes, and furniture parts, but not firewood. Various wildlife appreciate the buds, bark, and foliage.

Basswood

The northern American basswood and the southern white basswood are also called the "bee tree" because of the attraction their flowers have for bees. Their soft wood is often used for boxes, furniture, and pulpwood. The early colonists and the Native Americans made rope from the fibrous inner bark.

American Beech

This beech can grow as high as eighty feet and bears an edible nut eaten by wildlife and used by farmers to fatten pigs; it provides excellent firewood.

Birch

The birches on your property are easily identified by bark that comes away in papery strips. The two important birches are the yellow birch, also known as the gray, or silver, birch, and the paper birch, also called the canoe, or white, birch.

An example of selective thinning among young oaks and a few maples. A carpet of ferns under young trunks often indicates a previous fire.

The straight-grained hardwood of the yellow birch is used for furniture, veneers, floorboards, and boxes, and is a good firewood. The bark of the paper birch was used by the Native Americans for their lightweight canoes. Its wood now makes toothpicks, clothespins, toys, and pulpwood. One might also find sweet birch, with its dark, smooth bark that can be tapped in the spring to make birch beer.

Cedar

Red cedar is an aromatic wood, highly resistant to decay. It often is made into poles, posts, railroad ties, and shingles, and used as well in chests and closets to keep out moths and other insects. The Alaskan Indians hollowed out the trunks of red cedar to make canoes.

Black Cherry

This native tree grows across the eastern half of the United States. Its wood is valued for its beautifully varied grain and deep red color when polished. Early cabinetmakers often used it for tables and paneling. Wild cherry cough syrup is made from its bark.

Cottonwood

This is a fast-growing species valuable during pioneer days on the prairies and plains because it provided shade, timber, and firewood. Today it is often planted for shade and its wood is employed in crates, plywood, and pulpwood.

Western Hemlock

This tall hemlock can grow to 150 feet and is a familiar sight in the Pacific Northwest. It is an important pulpwood and provides cellulose for rayon yarns and plastics.

Hickory

The wood of the mockernut hickory and its related species is very hard and valued for tools, baseball bats, veneer, floorboards, furniture, and for smoking meats. It makes great firewood.

American Holly

Beautiful as an ornamental with its shiny green leaves and red berries, the American holly has a satiny wood often used for furniture inlays.

Maple

The most important eastern maple is the sugar maple, sometimes called the hard, or rock, maple. The wood is smooth and hard with a fine texture and has long been a favorite for furniture as well as flooring. This maple provides the wonderful sap that is boiled down to make maple syrup. In the Pacific Northwest the bigleaf maple, a handsome shade tree with wood used for veneer and furniture, has sap for syrup. Maple is a top-grade firewood.

Oak

There are so many different oaks that you are certain to find one or two varieties on your property. There are two main groups: white oaks have pale bark and rounded leaves, black oaks have darker bark and pointed leaves. All oaks have one thing in common — the production of acorns. The white oak is perhaps the best known because over time it can grow to be very large with heavy, hard wood. It was the first choice for ships, barns, and bridges, and is still used to make barrels for wine and whiskey. In hard times the acorns were eaten, roasted to make coffee, and ground into meal for bread.

Pecan

The pecan tree, originally wild, is now cultivated extensively for its nuts. Its wood is hard and tough. It is used for furniture, floorboards, and veneer as well as for firewood and smoking meat.

Pine

Now grown in plantations expressly for pulp, pine is a softwood. When the first settlers came to this country, various pines gave them the material for everything from houses, furniture, bridges, and barns to pitch, paints, tar, resin, turpentine, and fuel. Later, when eastern white pine became scarce, it was replaced by western white pine. Other pines of interest are the longleaf pine of the Southeast, tapped for turpentine and resin and logged for building; the ponderosa, the most commercially important pine of the West; the western lodgepole, used for mine timbers, posts, pulpwood, and lumber; and the shortleaf, or southern yellow, pine, good for construction and pulpwood. Pine produces too many sparks and too much creosote to make good firewood.

Saguaro

This giant tree cactus of the hot, dry Southwest has a woody interior framework that supplies material for shelters, fences, and kindling. The fruit of the saguaro has long been used for preserves, and its seeds provide food for birds.

Sweet gum

Sweet gums grow in the South, where they are an important hardwood timber tree. Sweet gum is used for furniture, veneer, plywood, pulpwood, and barrels. In earlier times a gum for medicinal purposes and chewing was obtained from the resin inside the bark.

Sycamore

A large shade tree, the sycamore grows in the eastern half of the country on old disturbed sites. Its wood is used for furniture, flooring, butcher block, and pulpwood.

Black Walnut

This native hardwood is now so scarce and valuable that one sometimes reads newspaper articles about thieves who chain-saw and steal walnut trees in the night. In earlier times it was plentiful and settlers used it for furniture and paneling. The nuts have an excellent meat and their hulls were once used to dye cloth dark brown.

Willows like those below supplied the flexible branches for wattle fencing.

Willow

Black willow, the largest native willow, grows in the eastern half of the country and can reach a size that makes it suitable for commercial purposes. It is used for furniture, cabinetwork, and pulpwood, and in colonial times was a source of charcoal for gunpowder. The basket, or osier, willow, introduced into this country by the early settlers, has flexible branches excellent for basket making and wickerwork.

Extensively used willows in France in what was Corot country.

I miss the elms. They gradually began to disappear when I was young, and by the time I got to America they had gone from here, too. They died from the activities of a beetle carrying a deadly fungus. First recognized in Holland over fifty years ago, there is still no defense against this virulent disease. It seems that over five hundred years ago an epidemic came and went. I read somewhere that farmers then removed sections of bark as a hoped-for cure.

The elm is hard to describe, being like one tree piled on top of another. Elm wood was always valuable but difficult to work. It never seemed to dry out, yet became the choice for keels and gunwales of ships, wharves, farm buildings, coffins, the wheel-hubs of carts, even early waterpipes. It was very much at home in the damp. My grandmother had a comb-backed elm armchair that I could barely lift. It would dry to a whiteness some time after being scrubbed.

When I saw this eight-inch-high leaf of winter kale in our garden, it looked like a minature cross section of a hundred-foot-tall common elm. Thinking about this, I remember what happened to the farming landscape. Elms had always been hedge trees. When diseased elms had to be cut and burned, the hedges went with them. I did the painting above from a memory I had of their disappearance; just the oaks remained, and the ghost of the hedgerow succeeded by stakes and barbed wire.

Rows of freshly cut hay waiting for the binder.

Haymaking, before harvest, is the first real summer activity that concerns the country community. After all, the farm animals have to be fed later in the year when they can't forage for themselves.

The weather is usually very active in midsummer when the tall grass is ready for mowing, and the cutting and baling of hay must be done before the rain spoils it. Often all the family, friends, and neighbors pitch in during the brief windows of opportunity between showers. Fresh and green hay will keep its nutrients if dry, but if baled damp, hay will rot and be useless.

I remember that when my wife and I were visiting friends in County Clare in early summer we were put to work with everyone else. As the mown hay was gathered into bales, we had to pile these into stacks to create the smallest target for the inevitable Irish rain. That day happened to be the longest of the year, with blue skies, a breeze and enough light for us to work until eleven p.m. So rare was this occasion, and so valuable the crop, that we even had time to get most of it under cover in the stone barn before dark. At suppertime we watched television and the big news of the day featured stories from all over Ireland about tractors overheating from the

A local contractor cuts hay for friends of mine.

uncommonly long hours on the job. We were glad to have been part of an event that was happening all over the country that day. I remember, too, that haymaking may be more frantic than wheat harvesting, but it was easier and lighter work. In the old days, lifting sheaves of wheat and stacking them into stooks was hard and heavy for a youngster. The stalks were sharp and slippery, and my young arms wrapped around them could barely retain the load before it slipped down and out of control. No wonder the harvesters celebrated when all was gathered in.

Looking like big Tootsie Rolls wearing plastic raincoats, round bales of hay have taken over from the smaller, square bales in many places. Even uncovered, they present a small surface to the rain and can remain in the open for a long time.

The grower's weather

Not surprisingly, old weather lore, rhymes, and sayings deal either with the needs of mariners or farmers. What is surprising is that the odd line or two we remember (picked up even by Shakespeare) were already in the language of country folk and in verses written for their use. Here are a few — both old and new — beginning with the wind:

If New Year's Eve night the wind blowth south,
It betokeneth warmth and growth;
If West, much milk and fish in the sea;
If North, much cold and storms there will be;
If East, the trees will bear much fruit;
If North-east, flee it, man and brute.

Though winds do rage, as winds were wood,
And cause spring tides to raise great flood,
And lofty ships leave anchor in mud,
Bereaving many of life, and of blood;
Yet true it is, as cow chews cud,
And trees, at spring, do yield forth bud,
Except wind stands, as never it stood,
It is an ill wind turns none to good.

North winds send hail, South winds bring rain,
East winds we bewail, West winds blow amain:
North-east is too cold, South-east not too warm,
North-west is too bold, South-west doth no harm.

The North is a noyer to grass of all suits,
the East a destroyer to herb and all fruits;
The South, with his showers, refresheth the corn,
the West, to all flowers, may not be forborne.

The West, as a father, all goodness doth bring,
the East, a forbearer no manner of thing;
The South, as unkind, draweth sickness too near,
the North, as a friend, maketh all again clear.

With temperate wind, we be blessed of God,
with tempest we find, we are beat with his rod:
All power, we know, to remain in his hand,
how ever wind blow, by sea or by land.

The Properties of Winds by Thomas Tusser

Snow is beneficial to the ground in winter, as it prevents its freezing to so great a depth as it otherwise would.
It guards the winter grain and other vegetables in a considerable degree from the violence of sudden frosts and from piercing and drying winds. The later snow lies on the ground in spring, the more advantage do grasses and other plants receive from it. Where a bank of snow has lain very late, the grass will sprout, and look green earlier, than in parts of the same field which were sooner bare.

From *The New England Farmer* by Samuel Deane

January blossoms fill no man's cellar.

A January spring is good for nothing.

A foot deep of rain
Will kill hay and grain;
But three feet of snow
Will make them grow mo.'

A dry May and a rainy June
Puts the farmer's pipe in tune.

If apples bloom in March,
In vain for 'em you'll sarch;
If apples bloom in April,
Why then they'll be plentiful;
If apples bloom in May,
You may eat 'em night and day.

A good deal of rain on Easter Day,
Gives a crop of grass but little good hay.

About the seasons of the year;
Astrologers may make a fuss:
But this I know, that Spring is here
When I cut asparagus.

Concerning dates, whate'er they pen
No matter whether true or not
I know it must be Summer when
Green peas are in the Pot.

And Autumn takes his turn to reign
I know as sure as I'm a sinner
When leaves are scattered o'er the plain
And grapes are eaten after dinner.

Winter is known by frost and snow,
To all the little girls and boys;
But it's enough for me to know,
I get no greens except savoys.

From *Poor Robin's Almanac*, 1808

If you can sit on the earth with your trousers down and it feels
all right, then sow your barley and it will be up in three nights.

Sow corn when the moon is waxing, never when it is waning.

A damp, warm March will bring much harm to the farm.

If the blackberry comes into flower in early June,
then an early harvest can be expected soon.

The wisdom of Thomas Tusser

Most gardening books are published in early spring. It seems understandable because that is when most gardeners order their seeds, start their seedlings, and take a look outside. But the farming and gardening year really starts in the fall. With some relatively easy work in the autumn we can save ourselves future fruitless battles and watch our plants flourish during the next growing season.

A bestseller was published in 1557, with the snappy title of *The Hundred Points of Good Husbandry*. The author was Thomas Tusser, a farmer living on the Suffolk/Essex border, an area still rich and productive. Following its success, Tusser amplified it to *The Five Hundred Points of Good Husbandry*. This book is the origin of many country sayings and quotations because Farmer Thomas had something of agricultural relevance to say for every day of the year. These snippets survive as easy-to-remember couplets or quatrains because each of the points is in verse. Verse is easy to remember, though its instruction may be hard to follow; in the 16th century it was a common form of communication. Tusser's work is certainly not poetry and barely qualifies as verse, but his rhymes speak from his heart and, most importantly, his experience.

We do not know how good a farmer Tusser was, but we do know that he was a conscientious scholar of farming, growing, and how things should be done on the farm. Like Thomas Jefferson, he was interested in theory and experiment. In the end, Tusser fell into debt as a farmer, leaving money owed him as his only bequest. His real legacy is his verse, full of charm and the rhythms of the growing seasons.

I had first thought of quoting brief pieces of Tusser as others have done, but then I thought that we should let Tusser talk us through the farming year. Here are about eighty of his points. I have taken the liberty of editing out of the original those not relevant to today's life or our different climatic regions. For instance, there was much about hemp and flax for making one's own linen, and the culture of hops for beer, the staple drink of Tusser's time. But these remaining points can be enjoyed and savored. I have also added a few annotations to make some of the 16th-century terms more easily understood.

From beginning to end I treat the whole trip through the points like a long satisfying walk across the fields on a cold day, and then to sit by the fire and go through the year again. So, like a good gardening book should, it opens with the ending of harvest and the beginning of preparations for the forthcoming growing season.

Tusser country. A willow and wild turnip on opposite banks of the River Stour, a couple of miles up from where he farmed.

Harvest into Fall

Dry August and warm, doth harvest no harm.

AUGUST

Make suer of reapers, get harvest in hand,
the corn that is ripe, do but shed as it stand:
Be thankful to God, for his benefits sent,
and willing to save it, with earnest intent.

Tip the foreman

Grant harvest lord, more, by a penny or two,
to call on his fellows the better to do:
Give gloves to thy reapers, a largess to cry,
and daily to loiterers have a good eye.

*Shock: sixty
sheaves of corn*

Gove: put

Reap well scatter not, gather clean that is shorn,
bind fast, shock apace, have an eye to thy corn;
Load safe, carry home, follow time being fair,
gove just in the barn, it is out of despair.

*Cocks:
conical heaps*

The mowing of barley, if barley do stand,
is cheapest and best, for to rid out of hand:
Some mow it, and rake it, and set it on cocks,
some mow it, and bind it, and set it on shocks.

Dallops: clumps

Of barley, the longest and greenest ye find,
leave standing by dallops, till time ye do bind:
Then early in morning, while dew is thereon,
to making of bands, till the dew be all gone.

Grutch: grudge

Where barley is raked, (if dealing be true),
the tenth of such raking to parson is due;
Where scattering of barley is seen to be much,
there custom nor conscience tithing should grutch.

Lubbers: idiots

If weather be fair, and tidy they grain,
make speedily carriage, for fear of a rain;
For tempest and showers deceiveth a many,
and lingering lubbers lose many a penny.

Blythe: joy

In harvest-time, harvest-folk, servants and all,
should make, all together, good cheer in the hall;
And fill out the black bowl of blythe to their song,
and let them be merry all harvest-time long.

Once ended thy harvest, let none be beguil'd,
please such as did help thee, man, woman, and child,
Thus doing, with alway, such help as they can,
thou winnest the praise of the labouring man

September blow soft, Till fruit be in loft.

SEPTEMBER

Thresh seed, and to fanning, September doth cry,
get plough to the field, and be sowing of rye:
To harrow the ridges, ere ever ye strike,
is one piece of husbandry Suffolk doth like.

Sow timely thy white-wheat, sow rye in the dust,
let seed have his longing, let soil have her lust:
Let rye be partaker of Michelmas spring,
to bear out the hardness that winter doth bring.

Though beans be in sowing, but scattered in,
yet wheat, rye, and peason, I love not too thin;
Sow barley and dredge with a plentiful hand,
lest weed stead of seed, overgroweth thy land.

Peason: peas
Dredge: to cast

No sooner a sowing, but out by and by,
with mother or boy, that alarum can cry;
And let them be armed with sling or with bow,
to scare away pigeon, the rook, and the crow

Fruit gathered too timely will taste of the wood,
will shrink and be bitter, and seldom prove good:
So fruit that is shaken, and beat off a tree,
with bruising in falling, soon faulty will be.

At Michelmas, safely, go stye up thy boar,
lest straying abroad, ye do see him no more:
The sooner the better for Hallontide nigh,
and better he brawneth, if hard he do l.

*Hallontide:
All Saint's Day, November i*

For rooting of pasture, ring hog ye had need,
which being well ringled, the better do feed.
Though young with their elders will lightly keep best,
yet spare not to ringle both great and the rest.

Ringled: enclosed

Keep hog, I advise thee, from meadow and corn,
for out aloud crying, that ere he was born:
Such lawless, so haunting, both often and long,
if dog set him chaunting, he doth thee no wrong.

Chaunting: squealing

Get home with thy brakes ere an summer be gone,
for teddered cattle, to sit thereupon.
To cover thy hovel, to brew and to bake,
to lie in the bottom, where hovel ye make.

*Brakes: bracken
— used for bedding
and for firing
bread ovens*

Fall into Winter

Now saw out thy timber, for board and for pale,
to have it unshaken, and ready for sale:
Bestow it, and stick it, and lay it aright,
to find it in March, to be ready in plight.

Slap: bark Save slap of thy timber, for stable and stye,
for horse and for hog, the more cleanly to lie;
Save saw-dust and brick-dust, and ashes so fine,
for alley to walk in, with neighbor of thine.

OCTOBER *October good blast, to blow the hog mast.*

Now lay up they barley-land, dry as ye can,
whenever ye sow it, so look for it than:
Get daily beforehand, be never behind,
lest winter preventing, do alter thy mind.

Green rye in September, when timely thou hast,
October for wheat-sowing calleth as fast:
If weather will suffer, this counsel I give,
leave sowing of wheat, before Hallowmas eve.

Harms: anger Who soweth in rain, he shall reap it with tears,
who soweth in harms, he is ever in fears:
Who soweth ill seed, or defraudeth his land,
Coresie: trouble hath eye-sore abroad, with a coresie at hand.

Sow acorns, ye owners that timber do love,
Haw: seed-head sow haw and rye with them, the better to prove:
Coney: rabbit If cattle or coney may enter to crop,
young oak is in danger, of losing his top.

Good bread-corn and drink-corn full twenty weeks kept,
is better than new, that at harvest is reapt
Bowd: weevils But foisty the bread-corn, and bowd-eaten malt,
for health or for profit, find noisome thou shalt.

November take flail; Let ship no more sail. NOVEMBER

At Hallontide, slaughter-time entereth in,
and then doth the husbandman's feasting begin:
From thence unto Shrovetide, kill now and then some,
their offall for household the better will come.

Such wheat as ye keep, for the baker to buy,
unthreshed till March, in the sheaf let it lie;
Lest foistiness take it, if sooner ye thresh it, *Foistiness: mildew*
although by oft turning, ye seem to refresh it.

Save chaff of the barley, of wheat, and of rye,
from feathers and foistiness, where it doth lie;
Which mixed with corn, being sifted of dust,
go give to thy cattle, when serve them ye must

Now plough up thy headland, or delve it with spade,
where otherwise profit but little is made;
And cast it up high, upon hillocks to stand.
that winter may rot it, to compost thy land.

The chimney all sooty, would now be made clean,
for fear of mischances, too oftentimes seen:
Old chimney and sooty, if fier once take,
by burning and breaking, some mischief may make.

When ploughing is ended, and pasture not great,
then stable thy horses, and tend them with meat.
Let season be dry, when ye take them to house,
for danger of nits, or for fear of a louse.

Lay compost up, handsomely, round on a hill,
to walk in thy yard, at thy pleasure and will;
More compost it maketh, and handsome the plot,
if horse-keeper, daily, forgetteth it not.

O dirty December, for Christmas remember. DECEMBER

Give cattle their fodder in plot dry and warm, *Miring: stuck*
and count them for miring, or other like harm: *on mudflats*
Young colts with thy wennels together go serve, *Wennels: weaned calves*
lest lurched by others, they happen to starve. *Lurched: pushed out*

The housing of cattle, while winter doth hold,
is good for all such as are feeble and old:
It saveth much compost, and many a sleep,
and spareth the pasture for walk of thy sheep.

Serve rye-straw out first, then wheat-straw and pease,
then oat-straw and barley, then hay if ye please:
But serve them with hay, while the straw stover last,
then love they no straw, they had rather to fast!

Yokes, forks, and such other, let bailiff spy out,
and gather the same, as he walketh about;
And after, at leisure, let this be his hire,
to beath them and trim them, at home by the fier.

Winter

Good fruit and good plenty cloth well in the loft,
then make thee an orchard, and cherish it oft;
For plant or for stock, lay aforehand to cast,
but set, or remove it, ere Christmas be past.

Look well to thy horses in stable thou must,
that hay be not foisty, nor chaff full of dust;
Nor stone in their provender, feather, nor clots,
Bots: maggots, worms   nor fed with green peason, for breeding of bots.

If frost do continue, take this for a law,
the strawberries look to be covered with straw,
Crotches: sticks, twigs   Laid overly trim upon crotches and bows,
and after uncovered, as weather allows.

JANUARY   *A kindly good January, freezeth pot by the fire.*

When Christmas is ended, bid feasting adieu,
go play the good husband, thy stock to renew,
Be mindful of rearing, in hope of a gain,
dame profit shall give thee reward for thy pain.

If frost do continue, this lesson doth well,
for comfort of cattle, the fuel to fell:
From every tree the superfluous boughs,
Neat: cattle   now prune for thy neat, thereupon to go browse.

Prie: privet   Lop poplar and sallow, elm, maple, and prie;
well saved from cattle, till summer to lie;
So far as in lopping, their tops ye do fling,
so far, without planting, young coppice will spring.

From Christmas, till May be well entered in,
some cattle ware faint, and look poorly and thin;
And chiefly when prime grass at first doth appear,
then most is the danger of all the whole year.

Take verjuice and heat it, a pint for a cow,
bay salt, a handfull, to rub tongue ye wot how: *Verjuice:*
That done, with the salt, let her drink off the rest;   *sour apple*
this many times raiseth the feeble up best.   *vinegar*

Young broom, or good pasture thy ewes do require   *Broom:*
warm berth, and in safety, their lambs do desire: *a heatherlike*
Look often well to them, for foxes and dogs,   *shrub*
for pits, and for brambles, for vermin, and hogs.

More dainty the lamb, the more worth to be sold,
the sooner the better, for ewe that is old;
But if ye do mind, to have milk of the dame,
till May, do not sever the lamb fro the same.

Ewes, yearly by twinning, rich masters do make,
the lamb of such twinners, for breeders go take:
For twinlings be twiggers, increase for to bring,   *Peccantem:*
though some of their twigging, peccantem may sing.   *a confession of error*

Sows ready to farrow this time of the year,
are for to be made of, and counted full dear.
For now is the loss of a fare of the sow,
more great than the loss of two calves of thy cow.

Of one sow, together, rear few above five,
and those of the fairest, and likest to thrive.   *Before: the strongest*
Ungelt, of the best keep a couple for store,   *piglet gets the front teats*
one boar pig and sow pig, that sucketh before.

Good milch cow, well fed, and that is fair and sound.
is yearly for profit, as good as a pound:
And yet by the year, have I proved ere now
as good to the purse, is a sow as a cow.

FEBRUARY

Feb, fill the dike, with what thou dost like.

Go plow in the stubble, take timely this season
for sowing of vetches of beans and of peason.
Now sooner ye sow them the sooner they come
And better for household they fill up a room.

Where banks be amended, and newly up-cast,
sow mustard-seed, after a shower be past,
Where plots full of nettles be noisome to eye,   *Noisome: offensive*
sow thereupon hemp-seed, and nettle will die.

Land-meadow that yearly is spared for hay,
now fence it and spare it, and dung it ye may.
Get mole-catcher cunningly mole for to kill,
and harrow, and cast abroad every hill.

Good provender, labouring horses would have,
good hay and good plenty, plough-oxen do crave;
To hale out thy muck, and to plow up thy ground,
or else it may hinder thee many a pound.

Winter into Spring

MARCH   *March dust to be sold, worth ransom of gold.*

In March is good grafting, the skilfull do know,
so long as the wind in the east do not blow:
From moon being changed, till past be the prime,
for grafting and cropping, is very good time.

Cropping: pruning

Things graffed or planted, the greatest and least,
defend against tempest, the bird, and the beast;
Defended shall prosper, the tother is lost,
the thing with the labour, the time and the cost.

Sow barley in March, in April, and May,
the later in sand, and the sooner in clay.
What worser for barley, than wetness and cold?
what better to skilfull, than time to be bold?

Who soweth his barley too soon, or in rain,
of oats of thistles shall after complain:
I speak not of May-weed, of Cockle and such,
that noieth the barley, so often and much.

Noieth: harms

Some rolleth their barley, straight after a rain,
when first it appeareth, to level it plain:
The barley so used, the better doth grow,
and handsome ye make it, at harvest to mow.

Oats, barley, and pease, harrow after you sow;
for rye, harrow first, as already ye know:
Leave wheat little clod, for to cover the head,
that after a frost, it may out and go spread.

If clod in thy wheat, will not break with the frost,
if now ye do roll it, it quiteth the cost;
But see when ye roll it, the weather be dry,
or else it were better, unrolled to lie.

Quiteth: reduce

Land falling or lying full south or south-west,
for profit by tillage, is lightly the best:
So garden with orchard and hop-yard I find,
that want the like benefit, grow out of kind.

At spring (for the summer) sow garden ye shall,
at harvest (for winter) or sow not at all,
Oft digging, removing, and weeding (ye see)
makes herb the more wholesome, and greater to be.

Now leeks are in season, for pottage full good,
and spareth the milch-cow, and purgeth the blood:
These having with peason, for pottage in Lent,
thou sparest both oat meal, and bread to be spent.

Sweet April showers, do spring May flowers.

APRIL

Look now, to provide ye of meadow for hay,
if fens be undrowned, there cheapest ye may;
In fen for the bullock, for horse not so well,
count best, the best cheap, wheresoever ye dwell.

Save elm, ash, and crab tree, for cart and for plough,
save step for a stile, of the crotch of the bough:
Save hazel for forks, save sallow for rake;
save hulver and thorn, thereof flail to make.

*Sallow: willow
Hulver: holly*

Allowance of fodder, some countries do yield,
as good for the cattle as hay in the field.
Some mow up their headlands and plots among corn,
and driven to leave nothing, unmown or unshorn.

Where stones be too many, annoying thy land,
make servant come home, with a stone in his hand:
By daily so doing, have plenty ye shall,
both handsome for paving, and good for a wall.

Spring into Summer

MAY *Cold May and windy, barn filleth up finely.*

In May get a weed-hook, a crotch and a glove,
and weed out such weeds, as the corn do not love.
For weeding of winter corn, now it is best;
but June is the better for weeding the rest.

Slack never thy weeding, for dearth nor for cheap,
the corn shall reward it, ere ever ye reap;
And specially where ye do trust for to seed,
let that be well used, the better to speed.

Twifallow: Twifallow once ended, get tumbrell and man,
plow twice and compost that fallow, as soon as ye can.
Let skilfull bestow it, where need is upon;
more profit the sooner, to follow thereon.

Pinch never thy wennels of water or meat,
if ever ye hope for to see them good neat.
In summer-time, daily; in winter, in frost,
if cattle lack drink, they be utterly lost.

Fine basil desireth it may be her lot,
Gilliflower: to grow as the gilliflower, trim in a pot;
a clove scented That ladies and gentles, to whom ye do serve,
flower may help her, as needeth, poor life to preserve.

Calm weather in June, corn sets in tune.

Wash sheep (for the better) where water doth run, JUNE
and let him go cleanly, and dry in the sun:
Then shear him, and spare not, at two days an end,
the sooner the better, his corps will amend.

If meadow be forward, be mowing of some,
but mow as the makers may well overcome.
Take heed to the weather, the wind, and the sky
so if danger approacheth, then cock apace, cry. *Cock apace:*
quickly

Plough early till ten a'clock, then to thy hay,
in plowing and carting, so profit ye may.
By little and little thus doing ye win,
that plough shall not hinder, when harvest comes in.

So likewise a hovell will serve for a room,
to stack on the peason, when harvest shall come;
And serve thee in winter moreover than that,
to shut up thy porklings, thou mindest to fat.

At midsummer, down with the brambles and brakes,
and after, abroad, with thy forks and thy rakes.
Set mowers a mowing, where meadow is grown,
the longer now standing, the worse to be mown.

No tempest, good July, lest corn look ruly. JULY

With tossing and raking, and setting on cocks,
grass lately in swathes, is hay for an ox:
That done, go and cart it, and have it away,
the battle is fought, ye have gotten the day.

Not rent off, but cut off, ripe bean with a knife,
for hindering stalk, of her vegetive life.
So gather the lowest, and leaving the top,
shall teach thee a trick, for to double thy crop.

Get grist to the mill, to have plenty in store,
lest miller lack water, as many do more.
The meal the more yieldeth, if servant be true,
and miller that tolleth, take none but his due.

Conclusion

The land can be made to produce amazing results for those willing to
work at it. John Seymour, the author of *Farming for Self-Sufficiency,*
mentioned that the Israelis, formerly urban people — city dwellers *par excellence*
— have performed wonders in turning their hard-baked soil into farmland.
One of their pioneering agriculturists said that if you have a lot
of sun and sand, all that's needed is irrigation and the right fertilizing.
And up on the once barren hills between Tel Aviv and Jerusalem, believers in
nature's power planted thousands of trees that produced cover, shade, timber,
even a mini-climate change, and of course, culture.

Henry David Thoreau, his classic *Walden*, and his two-year experience living alone
on the edge of Walden Pond, remains our most potent literary symbol of the
desire for self-sufficiency. But without attempting to be completely self-sufficient
or (like the Israelis) changing the desert into a garden, we can have a varied
life and diet by planting enough and by using what nature itself grows and
provides around us. We know that the return to country living has coincided with
the decline of the family farm. In a way that I find sad and moving,
the abandoned, uncultivated countryside becomes more beautiful with
the return of wildflowers, woods, and wildlife.

After dealing with the domestic side of country living: the house, the outbuildings
the livestock, and the fields, I think we should explore the proper balance between
the right amount of cultivation and what we leave untouched and overgrown — to
me the most interesting and the least known topic. The forager and gatherer in me
wants to find out all I can about edible and medicinal plants, the value of trees
while they continue to grow, the resident birds and animals, and
all that the Native Americans told us and was then forgotten —
the wild side of country wisdom.

A Brief Chronology of American Farming

1600s-late 1700s Oxen and horses for power, crude wooden plows, all sowing by hand, cultivating by hoe, hay and grain cutting with sickle, threshing with flail.

1600s-1700s Native foods introduced to the colonists included maize, pumpkins, gourds, squashes, pecans, black walnuts, maple sugar, and tobacco; okra and peanuts brought by African slaves.

1700s English farmers settled in New England villages; Dutch, German, Swedish, Scotch-Irish, and English farmers settled on isolated Middle Colony farmsteads; English and some French farmers settled on plantations in tidewater and on isolated Southern Colony farmsteads in the Piedmont; Spanish settled the Southwest and California.

1790s Cradle scythe introduced.

1790 Total population: 3,929,214; farmers made up about 90 percent of the labor force; the U.S. area settled extended westward an average of 255 miles; parts of the frontier crossed the Appalachians.

1795-1815 Sheep industry in New England at its height.

1796 Public Land Act of 1796 authorized federal land sales to the public in minimum 640-acre plots at $4 of credit per acre.

1797 Charles Newbold patented first cast-iron plow.

1815-25 Competition with western farm areas began to force New England farmers out of wheat and meat production.

1830s Some 250-300 hours of labor required to produce 100 bushels (5 acres) of wheat with walking plow, brush harrow, hand broadcast of seed, sickle, and flail; McCormick reaper patented.

1837 John Deere and Leonard Andrus began making steel plows; practical threshing machine patented.

1840-60 Rural buldings improved with introduction of the balloon frame construction.

1842 First grain elevator, Buffalo, N.Y. Practical mowing machine patented.

1845-55 Potato famine in Ireland, German Revolution of 1848 greatly increased immigration to U.S.

1850s Successful farming on the prairies began.

1850 Total population 23,191,786; farmers made up 64 percent of labor force; number of farms 1,449,000; average acres 203; 75-90 hours of labor required to produce 100 bushels of corn (2 1/2 acres) with walking plow, harrow, and hand planting.

1854 Self-governing windmill perfected.

1856 Two-horse straddle-row cultivator patented.

1860s Total population 31,443,321; farmers made up 58 percent of labor force, average acres 199; kerosene lamps became popular.

1862 Homestead Act granted 160 acres to settlers who had worked the land for five years.

1862-75 Change from hand power to horses characterized the first American agricultural revolution.

1865-90 Sod houses common on the prairies.

1866-77 Cattle boom accelerated settlement of Great Plains; range wars between farmers and ranchers.

1866-86 The days of the cattlemen on the Great Plains.

1868 Experimentation with steam tractors.

1869 Spring-tooth harrow for seedbed preparation appeared.

1870s Silos came into use.

1870 Total population 38,558,371; farmers made up 53 percent of labor force; number of farms 2,660,000; average acres 153.

1874 Glidden patented barbed wire. Availability of barbed wire allowed fencing of rangeland, ending era of unrestricted, open-range grazing.

1874-76 Grasshopper plagues were serious in the West.

1880s Heavy agricultural settlement on the Great Plains began; most immigrants were from southeastern Europe; most humid land already settled.

1880 William Deering put 3,000 twine binders on the market.

1884-90 Horse-drawn combine used in Pacific Coast wheat areas.

1887-97 Drought reduced settlement on the Great Plains.

1890 Total population 62,941,714; farmers made up 43 percent of labor force; number of farms 4,565,000; average acres 136; 35-40 hours of labor required to produce 100 bushes (2 1/2 acres) of corn with 2-bottom gang plow, disk and peg-tooth harrow, and 2-row planter; 40-50 hours of labor required to produce 100 bushels (5 acres) of wheat with gang plow, seeder, harrow, binder, thresher, wagons, and horses.

1900-10 George Washington Carver, director of agricultural research at Tuskegee Institute, pioneered new uses for peanuts, sweet potatoes, and soybeans, thus helping to diversify southern agriculture.

1918 Small prairie combine with auxiliary engine introduced.

1932-36 Drought and dust-bowl conditions developed.

1940 Total population 131,820,000; farmers made up 18 percent of labor force; number of farms 6,102,000; average acres 175; one farmer supplied 10.7 persons.

1941-45 Frozen foods popularized.

1945-70 Change from horses to tractors and the adoption of a group of technological practices characterized the second American agricultural revolution; acreage of crops such as oats, required for horse and mule feed, dropped sharply as the use of tractors increased.

1945 Some 10-14 hours of labor required to produce 100 bushels (2 acres) of corn with tractor, 3-bottom plow, 10-foot tandem disk, 4-section harrow, 4-row planters and cultivators, and 2-row picker.

1950 One farmer supplied 15.5 persons.

1954 Number of tractors on farms exceeded the number of horses and mules for the first time.

1955 Some 6-12 hours of labor required to produce 100 bushels (4 acres) of wheat with tractor, 10-foot plow, 12-foot row weeder, harrow, 14-foot drill and self-propelled combine, and trucks.

1960 Total population 180,007,000; farmers made up 8.3 percent of the labor force; number of farms 3,711,000; average acres 303; one farmer supplied 25.8 persons; 96 percent of corn acreage now planted with hybrid seed.

1970 One farmer supplied 75.8 persons.

1980s More farmers used no-till or low-till methods to curb erosion.

1987 Some 3 hours of labor required to produce 100 bushels (3 acres) of wheat with tractor, 35-foot sweep disk, 30-foot drill, 25-foot self-propelled combine, and trucks; 2 3/4 hours of labor required to produce 100 bushels (1 1/8 acres) of corn with tractor, 5-bottom plow, 25-foot tandem disk, planter, 25-foot herbicide applicator, 15-foot self-propelled combine, and trucks.

1990 Total population 246,081,000; farmers made up 2.6 percent of the labor force; number of farms 2,143,150; average acres 461.

Bibliography

Angier, Bradford. *One Acre and Security.* New York: Vintage Books, 1973.

Baron, Robert C., ed. *The Garden and Farm Books of Thomas Jefferson.* Golden, Colorado: Fulcrum, Inc., 1987.

Belanger, Jerome D. *The Homesteader's Handbook to Raising Small Livestock.* Emmaus, Pennsylvania: Rodale Press Inc., 1974.

Courtauld, George. *An Axe, A Spade and Ten Acres.* London: Secker & Warburg, 1983.

Eisenberg, Evan. "Back to Eden." *The Atlantic Monthly,* November 1989.

Evans, George Ewart. *Ask the Fellows Who Cut the Hay.* London: Faber and Faber, 1961.

Evans, George Ewart. *The Crooked Scythe: An Anthology of Oral History.* London: Faber and Faber, 1993.

Foster, Gertrude. *Herbs for Every Garden.* New York: E.P. Dutton & Co., Inc., 1966.

Halsted, Byron D., ed. *Barns, Sheds and Outbuildings.* Lexington, Massachusetts: The Stephen Greene Press, 1977.

Harman, Tony. *Seventy Summers: The Story of a Farm.* London: BBC Books, 1986.

Hartley, Dorothy. *Lost Country Life.* London: Macdonald & Janes Publishers, Ltd., 1979.

Hartley, Dorothy, ed. *Thomas Tusser: His Good Points of Husbandry.* Bath: Country Life Limited, 1931.

Kains, M.G. *Five Acres and Independence.* New York: Dover Publications, Inc., 1973.

Klinkenborg, Verlyn. *Making Hay.* New York: Vintage Books, 1986.

Martin, George A. *Fences, Gates and Bridges.* New York: O. Judd Co., 1887.

Morton, H.V. *I Saw Two Englands.* Revisited and photographed by Tommy Candler. London: Methuen, 1989.

Muir, Richard and Nina. *Fields.* London: Macmillan London Limited, 1989.

Murkett, Peter, ed. *Monterey, A Local History.* Monterey, Massachusetts: The Town of Monterey, 1997.

Noble, Allen G. *To Build a New Land: Ethnic Landscapes in North America.* Baltimore: The Johns Hopkins Press, 1992.

_____. *Wood, Brick and Stone: Barns and Farm Structures.* Amherst: The University of Massachusetts Press, 1984.

Phillips, C.E. Lucas. *The Small Garden.* London: Pan Books Ltd., 1956.

Phillips, Roger, and Nicky Foy. *Herbs.* London: Pan Books Ltd., 1990.

Phillips, Roger, and Martyn Rix, *Vegetables.* London: Pan Books Ltd., 1993.

Pollan, Michael. *Second Nature: A Gardener's Education.* New York: Atlantic Monthy Press, 1991.

Seymour, John and Sally. *Farming for Self-Sufficiency.* New York: Schocken, 1973.

Simpson, Milt. *Windmill Weights.* Newark, New Jersey: Johnson & Simpson Graphic Designers, 1985.

Zube, Ervin H., ed. *Landscapes: Selected Writings of J.B. Jackson.* Amherst: University of Massachusetts Press, 1970.

Acknowledgments

I would like to thank the following for their help in the preparation of this book.

Chris and Edna Bergstrom; Tommy Candler and Alan Plaistow; Bridget Crawford; Steve Davis; Ronnie and Becky Dodd; Lorin Driggs; Denis Farina, Liza Fosburgh; Nicky Foy; Michael and Neyla Freeman; Doris Halle, John and Betty Holmes; Marc and Vivienne Jaffe; Ian Ross Jenkins and Maria Carvainis; James Kunkle; Anna Larkin; Kay Larkin; Sally Larkin; Terry McAweeny; Robert H. Robinson; Elaine and Paul Rocheleau; Anita Carroll-Weldon, Director of The Bidwell House Museum; the Zema family of Stephentown, New York; and the many farmers and gardeners who let me make a record of their work. Special thanks to Roger Phillips, fellow ex-art director, twenty years on since we collaborated on his first book; his photographs have revolutionized the way we look at plants. The decoration above the title on page 3 is an overmantel cresting in linden, carved by David Esterly in 1994 (photo: Ildiko Butler).

Photo Credits

Robert S. Arnold, Old Sturbridge Village, 74 *bottom.*

The Barn People, 35 *bottom* left.

Tommy Candler, 2, 6, 11, 13 *bottom*, 46-47, 56, 58 *bottom*, 59 *bottom*, 62, 63, 64, 66, 67, 68 *top*, 69, 70 *top and bottom*, 71, 79, 81, 85, 87, 96, 97, 102 *top*, 122, 125 *left and right*, 127 *left and right*, 131 *top left*, 136, 137, 138 *top and bottom*, 144 *top*, 147 *top*, 156.

Bruce Coleman Inc.: Jonathan Wright, 18, 19, 26 *left*, 50-51.

Gary Day-Ellison, 13 *top.*

Steve Davis, Living History Farms, 65.

Michael Freeman, 38, 39, 43 *bottom*, 44, 57, 58 *top*, 115 *top and bottom right*, 144 *bottom*, 148-140, 150.

Fred Hoogervorst, 22, 28, 29.

David Larkin, 4 *left and right*, 12, 15, 16, 20, 23, 26 *right*, 27, 30 *right*, 31, 32 *right*, 33 *top left*, 33 *bottom left and right*, 34 *left*, 35 *top*, 40, 45, 48, 49, 52, 53, 54, 55, 58 *middle*, 59 *top*, 60, 68 *bottom*, 74 *top*, 76, 77 *middle*, 78 *top, middle left and bottom*, 80, 84, 86, 89, 91, 93, 95, 99, 102 *bottom*, 103 *top*, 104 *bottom*, 105 *bottom*, 106 *left*, 108, 109, 115 *left and middle right*, 117 *top*, 128 *top*, 134 *left and right*, 135, 139 *top*, 145, 146, 147 *bottom.*

Harold E. Malde, 72-73 *top*, 73 *bottom.*

John Holmes, 77 *top, bottom left and right*, 78 *middle right.*

The New Jersey Barn Company, 32 *left*, 33 *top right*, 35 *bottom right.*

Roger Phillips, 88, 90, 92, 94, 98, 100, 101, 103 *bottom*, 104 *top*, 105 *top*, 106 *right*, 107, 110, 111, 112-113, 114, 116, 117 *bottom*, 118-119, 120-21, 123, 126, 128 *bottom*, 129, 130, 131 *top right and bottom left and right.*

Paul Rocheleau, 9, 21, 24-25, 34 *right*, 36, 37, 41, 42, 43 *top*, 61, 72 *bottom*, 75, 82-83, 123, 124, 132-133, 139 *bottom*, 140-141, 142-143.

William Sladcik, 30 *left.*